Songs I Love to Sing

MERRY CHRISTMAS

Dear Library and ARC Family:

This wonderful book serves as special recognition for you and your faithful ministry through the Billy Graham Library and Archive and Research Center, and as a historical reference for your greater understanding of Mr. Graham and his close associates. Another way to learn about BGEA music history is by reading and engaging this rich narrative.

Merry Christmas to you and your family!

With great appreciation, affection and prayer for you in Christ Jesus.

[signature]

Christmas 2023

SONGS I LOVE TO SING

The Billy Graham Crusades
and the Shaping of Modern Worship

EDITH L. BLUMHOFER

WILLIAM B. EERDMANS PUBLISHING COMPANY
GRAND RAPIDS, MICHIGAN

Wm. B. Eerdmans Publishing Co.
4035 Park East Court SE, Grand Rapids, Michigan 49546
www.eerdmans.com

29 28 27 26 25 24 23   1 2 3 4 5 6 7

ISBN 978-0-8028-7529-7

Library of Congress Cataloging-in-Publication Data

Names: Blumhofer, Edith Waldvogel author.
Title: Songs I love to sing : the Billy Graham crusades and the shaping of modern
    worship / Edith L. Blumhofer.
Description: Grand Rapids, Michigan : William B. Eerdmans Publishing Com-
    pany, 2023. | Includes bibliographical references and index. | Summary:
    "A history of the Billy Graham Crusades and the impact they made on the use
    of music in American worship services"—Provided by publisher.
Identifiers: LCCN 2022055933 | ISBN 9780802875297
Subjects: LCSH: Church music—Evangelical Church. | Church music—United
    States—20th century. | Graham, Billy, 1918–2018.
Classification: LCC ML3111.5 .B58 2023 | DDC 782.32/2995—dc23/eng/202211/18
LC record available at https://lccn.loc.gov/2022055933

CONTENTS

FOREWORD

On October 1, 2001, I flew from Orange County, California, up to Fresno where I had been invited to perform at a Billy Graham crusade. My bandmates and I were thrilled to be asked to participate in such an important event at such a tender moment as the nation—the entire world really—reeled from the attack on the World Trade Center and Pentagon not even three weeks earlier.

During that afternoon's sound check we could see armed SWAT officers in place on the roof and in the rafters of Bulldog Stadium. We were told that an AWAC aircraft would also be flying above us throughout the crusade to help protect the projected forty to sixty thousand people who would attend. The tension was palpable all day, though it was tempered for me by the great honor of playing for Billy Graham.

I grew up in the '60s when Billy Graham was already an internationally known evangelist. When my siblings and I were little kids and a crusade was going to be televised live, my mom would set out four television trays in front of the couch for us so that we could watch the event while we ate dinner. We knew and loved all the various players, especially George Beverly Shea and Cliff Barrows. And one of those TV-tray nights was the first time I heard Ethel Waters's amazing voice. I think she sang "His Eye Is on the Sparrow," though I can't be sure all these years later. Music was a huge part of Graham's ministry, and as a young pianist, his example drew me into the world of hymnody. In my wildest dreams I would never have imagined that one day I, too, would be a musical guest at one of those massive, sacred events.

While we played our brief set at Bulldog Stadium that evening, I turned around once between songs and saw many familiar faces hanging out in the backstage area—mostly celebrity pastors I knew from playing in churches over the years. I saw Billy Graham, too. He was in a wheelchair because he'd stubbed his toe in his hotel room the previous night. I believe he preached all three Fresno nights while sitting. We finished our set and I ran into Charlie Daniels as I walked off the stage. He told me that he liked my music and gave me a bear hug. Charlie was six feet two. I am five feet six. He pretty much lifted me off the ground and enthusiastically shook me back and forth, my feet dangling in the air like a Raggedy Andy doll.

A few years later I was leading worship for a retreat led by Anne Graham-Lotz at the Billy Graham Training Center—a.k.a. The Cove—in Asheville, North Carolina. Anne and I had become friends a decade earlier and we had traveled all over the world together—Paraguay, Panama, Puerto Rico, the Philippines, Korea, the UK, and many other places. I was delighted when Anne invited me to come have barbecue with "Mother and Daddy" the next afternoon. I was also terrified I might be asked to quote my favorite scriptures! I've never been any good at memorizing anything but Bach, Beethoven, Mozart, and Brahms, so I drove back to my cabin and opened up John's Gospel and tried to cram.

Thankfully, I was never asked to recite any scriptures the next day. Billy was again in a wheelchair, having been diagnosed with something akin to Parkinson's disease. Still, he was very engaged in our conversation, asking me all about my music ministry, where I'd played, whom I'd worked with. He was happy to learn that I'd gotten my start in the ministry through Campus Crusade for Christ, because he loved and respected its founder, Bill Bright. After our conversation, his energy flagging, Billy went to bed early, and I wound up eating barbecue at a small table in the kitchen with Anne and her spectacular mother, Ruth Bell Graham.

We talked about poetry, music, China, and Johnny Cash. She spoke of wild practical jokes the Graham family had played on each other over the years. The one that had me laughing the most involved one of the grandsons dumping a live fish into the other's swim trunks as he walked down the beach. The Graham grandsons are very tall, so the visual of one of those giants hopping around on the beach with a fish in his trunks was hilarious.

After we finished eating, Ruth wanted me to sing for her at the piano. She reclined on the sofa as I sang. Who gets to do that! It was dreamy. Afterward she took my hands in hers and asked me to promise I would sing for her funeral. Deeply touched, I told her I would be there.

The last time I saw Billy Graham was on his ninety-sixth birthday. Anne and I were again at The Cove and she told me the family was going to gather at Montreat after the seminar to have a brief devotion, sing "Happy Birthday," and eat cake. The devotion was led by Anne. Then one of the caretakers brought in the candlelit cake while we all sang. The gathering was short because Billy was tired. But before we all left, he asked me if I would sing for him. "Of course!" I replied, and I asked if we could go to the piano. He said, "Why don't you just come close to me and sing a cappella." I leaned in close to his ear and sang an original song, my knees quaking with the honor I was being given in that surreal moment.

My own relationship with Billy Graham has always been centered on music—as a child in front of the television, as a worship leader for his daughter Anne, as a guest soloist at the Fresno Crusade, and as a trembling minstrel at his birthday party. But music also looms large in the relationships hundreds of thousands of people have with Billy Graham. It played a vital, indispensable role in his ministry.

Music welcomed the vast throngs of people as they entered into the stadiums. Music tied all the elements of the service together, brought people to the altar, and then sent them back out into the world. While the importance of music is not unique to Billy Graham's ministry, the history of how it came to be is a fascinating and multifaceted story, as documented here in Edith Blumhofer's brilliantly researched and beautifully narrated book.

I was especially absorbed by Dr. Blumhofer's deft exploration of George Beverly Shea's and Cliff Barrows's early experiences with church music as children and their eventual influence on the crusades. Especially intriguing to me was the important role Moody Radio WMBI in Chicago had in launching the singing ministry of Shea. I have been a frequent guest on Moody Radio over the years and I've performed for several Friday Night Sings. There's a lot of history in that venerated old building on the Moody Institute campus that I was not aware of until I read this book.

Hymns and spiritual songs have always been and remain central in the Graham family and their various ministries around the world. And this book is a treasure trove for anyone who has loved the music of this era.

Foreword

Dr. Blumhofer approached her subject in the most scholarly way, obviously spending hours and hours on painstaking research. But her delivery is filled with respect and admiration, told in a friendly and accessible manner. This book is a gift.

Fernando Ortega

ACKNOWLEDGMENTS

My interest in the music of the Graham crusades reaches as far back as I can remember. Crusade recordings, Bev Shea records, and *Hour of Decision* broadcasts brought the music into our home, and my family sang along and enjoyed it together. When the Institute for the Study of American Evangelicals at Wheaton College received a grant from the Lilly Endowment to explore Billy Graham's role in Christianity, I accepted an assignment to prepare a conference paper on crusade music. It became a chapter in *Billy Graham: American Pilgrim* (2017). That was the beginning of this longer look at Graham crusade music.

Until the spring of 2019, the papers that enabled serious study of crusade music and the men whose principles shaped it resided at the Billy Graham Center Archives at Wheaton College, so as a Wheaton faculty member, I was well situated to delve deeply into the scrapbooks, recordings, correspondence, institutional records, and crusade records that charted the story. Other archives provided essential supporting materials, including the Bob Jones University Archives, which houses records of Cliff Barrows's student days and his later interactions with the school's leaders. George Beverly Shea proved more difficult to track. Since he was never a regular employee of the Billy Graham Evangelistic Association (BGEA), his papers and correspondence were not collated. His sister, Ruth Willett, and several nieces and nephews as well as his son, Ron Shea, patiently answered many questions and shared priceless family information. The Billy Graham Center Archives recently acquired boxes of Shea effects that remain unprocessed but contain priceless information. Houghton College Archives, the Wesleyan Church Archives in Indianapolis, and the

Acknowledgments

Wesleyan Church District Archives in Eastern Ontario make it possible to reconstruct much of Shea's childhood and the abiding influence of the Wesleyan Church on his character. Shea's Canadian friends around Winchester, Ontario, as well as Winchester Public Library personnel assisted in different ways. The Church of the Nazarene Archives holds some useful information about some crusade hymns.

The most important place for my research, though, was the Billy Graham Center Archives at Wheaton College, Wheaton, Illinois. In the 1980s, Billy Graham selected Wheaton as the repository for his materials, and he took a personal hand in articulating the policies that made the collection a world-class research gem. In the spring of 2019, that collection was abruptly moved to Charlotte, North Carolina, where it was held in storage and unavailable as I was working on this book. The archives staff at Wheaton College, especially Robert Shuster, Paul Ericksen, and Kathryn Graber, provided excellent service in the collections. The Billy Graham Center Archives presented a stellar environment in which to work and network with others who held like interests.

On the BGEA side of questions pertaining to Graham resources, David Bruce deserves mention for tireless efforts to make available the materials scholars needed. I am grateful as well to Ann Barrows, who allowed me to look among the treasures of her gracious home. And I recall with deep pleasure several interviews given to me by Cliff Barrows.

Shea's son, Ron, helped fill in gaps, as did Shea's sister, Ruth Willett, who shared a treasure trove of family materials at her home in Dahlonega, Georgia. The quest for Shea materials also led to several days of concentrated research in the Ottawa Valley, made possible by the hospitality of Marguerite van Die, professor emerita at the Queens University in Kingston, Ontario, and the kindness of independent scholar Alvyn Austin. I am grateful to the Reverend Laurence Croswell for providing access to historical records of the Wesleyan Church District Office in Canada as well as to some materials on Ralph Horner. The Shea roots in Canada led to some obscure Holiness sources like the Mooers Camp Meeting and other networks that constitute a little-known chapter in grassroots Ottawa Valley Protestant history. A Lilly Endowment grant to the Institute for the Study of American Evangelicals funded travel and research.

The archival staff at Bob Jones University, Greenville, South Carolina, proved helpful in every possible way and holds a small but rich trove of documents relating to Cliff and Billie (Wilma Newell) Barrows. It also has items pertaining to other early BGEA employees. Archivists at the Church of the Nazarene and those at the Wesleyan Church Archives outside Indianapolis provided invaluable help.

Over several years, various research assistants came alongside. Chief among them was Becky Baker, who began helping as an undergraduate assistant and finished as a Wheaton College employee. I could not have done much without Becky's abilities to pursue the nontraditional research required for this work. I am also grateful to my children, Jonathan, Judith, and Christopher, each of whom brought their own critical eye to this work.

This little book is dedicated to my husband, Edwin, who immersed himself with me in this story and is as taken by its characters and music as I am. When all is said and done, we both come away feeling much like Cliff Barrows: "This is *my* story, This is *my* song." The biographies of the songs chart the story of the crusades better than does that of any single life.

EDITOR'S PREFACE

The job of editing *Songs I Love to Sing*, the late Edith Blumhofer's manuscript on the music of the Billy Graham crusades, has been a bittersweet endeavor. I knew Edith for over thirty years and, for over twenty of those years, counted her as a colleague and friend while working with her at the Institute for the Study of American Evangelicals (ISAE) at Wheaton College. Her untimely passing in early 2020 was a profound tragedy for her family, friends, and former colleagues, but it was also a significant loss for the ongoing scholarly examination of American Protestant religion.

Edith Blumhofer was a gifted historian and writer with a wide-ranging expertise and set of interests that first manifested itself in meticulous scholarly work on early Pentecostalism and the history of the Assemblies of God. Her talents as a writer and relentless researcher, as well as her interest in the role of women within the history of American evangelicalism, were evidenced in Edith's critically acclaimed biographies of evangelist Aimee Semple McPherson (*Aimee Semple McPherson: Everybody's Sister*, Eerdmans, 1993) and the hymn writer Fanny Crosby (*Her Heart Can See: The Life and Hymns of Fanny J. Crosby*, Eerdmans, 2005). In her work with the ISAE, she helped conceive and then oversaw major projects on evangelical voluntary agencies, Pentecostalism, evangelical missions, Protestant hymnody, and the ministry of Billy Graham.

Edith's book on the music of the Billy Graham crusades joins her gift for biography with many of her larger historical interests, including hymnody and the history of evangelism. A number of volumes over the years have been devoted to Billy Graham's message, reception, image, and cultural context and importance. Edith conceived this project as a way to get at the vastly underestimated contribution that music played in undergirding Graham's message and appeal through the crusade experience—as encountered live or through media. She was particularly keen to bring George Beverly Shea and Cliff Barrows out from under Graham's enormous shadow and highlight the role they played in creating a setting that was an essential element of the crusades' success. In that effort, Edith hoped to convey the reality of Graham, Shea, and Barrows as *a team*—a team committed to one another and their task of reaching the world for Jesus.

When I began the task of editing the book, I found it, unsurprisingly, to already be a coherent manuscript not far from being ready for publication. The main challenge seemed to be fine-tuning all the diverse parts of the story that Edith had been trying to bring together: the stories of the Graham team members; the history of the BGEA; the "biographies" of the various hymns and gospel songs that played a key role in the crusades; the importance of well-loved "guest stars"; the diversity of the Graham team's various audiences; and the generational changes in musical styles and tastes. The story of crusade music was a complicated tale.

Fortunately, the story was well on its way to being told. There were a few places where rearranging sections helped the flow. I made a few adjustments that I believe help make the chronology of events easier to navigate. There were some instances of repetition that I tried to eliminate. At a few points I added explanatory or enhancing material that I believe Edith would likely have added herself had she been given the opportunity to finish the book. In the end, however, the completed product is truly her argument, her analysis, and for the very most part, her words.

One unfortunate difference between this manuscript and Edith's prior scholarly works is that its incomplete status and the timing of her passing meant that her specific references and endnotes had yet to be compiled. Given her reputation as a gifted and diligent researcher, the loss of Edith's detailed investigative trail behind *Songs I Love to Sing* is a loss for casual readers and scholars alike. Fortunately, her statements in this volume's acknowledgments section give us a good idea of where her research journey had already taken her, as do the endnotes she compiled for her chapter on the Graham team's music in a 2017 collection edited by Andrew Finstuen, Grant Wacker, and Anne Blue Wills: *Billy Graham: American Pilgrim* (Oxford). As an additional tool to assist those readers who want to dig deeper,

I have compiled a select bibliography that—across different points in time—provides insight into the stories of the Graham team, the history of the Graham organization, the lives of important musical contributors to the crusades, as well as background on the larger context of the evangelical subculture and its musical expressions.

As noted above, this project was a bittersweet assignment. As I worked on the manuscript, I was continually reminded of Edith's abilities as a researcher, writer, and historian, as well as her love for the hymns and gospel songs of the evangelical church. I was also keenly aware that the book would have been better had she been able to nip and tuck the final product to her satisfaction. Yet, under the circumstances, I was happy to be able to play a part in bringing her story of the music of the Billy Graham crusades past the finish line. My thanks to David Bratt of Eerdmans for approaching me for this task before he launched out on new career endeavors. Thanks also to James Ernest, Lisa Ann Cockrel, Laurel Draper, and Tom Raabe at Eerdmans for editorial help—and patience—in helping me wrap up my part of this process. Thanks to Edith's longtime friend Grant Wacker, emeritus professor at Duke Divinity School, for some encouraging words as I began the editorial process. Finally, thanks to Edith's husband, Ed, and to her son Chris Blumhofer for their very helpful efforts in retrieving some documents, lists, and notes from Edith's laptop.

—Larry Eskridge
McDowell County, North Carolina
July 29, 2022

PRELUDE

On Sunday afternoon, April 12, 1959, more than fifty thousand people crowded the Sydney (Australia) Showground to hear the American evangelist Billy Graham. As the service opened, reporters marveled at the hush that settled over the throng: "Billy Graham must be the only man these days who can demand absolute silence from a crowd . . . and get it," one wrote. The hush lasted through an "intensely moving" 2.5 hours until Graham at last brought things to a climax by speaking a simple invitation into a battery of microphones:

"Jesus hung naked and bleeding in front of a crowd for you. Certainly you can walk a few steps on this lovely afternoon to give your life to Him. You come!"

An electric organ, as yet barely audible, insinuated its way into the arena.

"The Bible warns not to put it off. It says now is the day of salvation! I'm going to ask hundreds of you to get up out of your seats wherever you are and come and stand reverently and quietly."

The organ music began to swell.

"Just get up, men, women and young people! We're going to wait. There's plenty of time."

Down near the front a middle-aged woman walked confidently to the rostrum. The ice was broken; decision rippled through the crowd like wind. Suddenly, the few turned into a flood.

The 1,000-voice choir had now joined the organ in "Just As I Am"— but not so loudly that Billy, far more persuasive than any electric organ, could not still be heard.

"There's a little voice down inside speaking to you. That's the Holy Spirit. This is your moment and hour. You'd better not miss it! This is it! You come!"

The choir sang on, repeating "Just as I Am" for twenty minutes and more until the movement forward finally ended with Graham's brief exhortation and benediction.

Several times during the invitation Graham stepped back from the microphone, crossed his arms, and silently waited. He remembered the singing of "Just as I Am" at the Mordecai Ham revival in Charlotte, North Carolina, where he had come forward twenty-five years earlier. He had not moved from his seat until the last notes of invitation music were fading, and so he always gave people time to begin coming. He knew just how long was required to reach the platform from the most distant spot in the stands. Before the first service in any new venue, one of his team arrived a few hours early to time that walk. Like everything else at Graham crusades, the invitation took everything into consideration: distance, crowding, and the inner struggles that made people hesitate.

A similar scene climaxed every service in the 417 crusades Graham conducted in 185 countries over nearly sixty years. Cliff Barrows directed the choir and organ in a way that complemented Graham's urgent words. Music and message harmonized completely: "Come." "Come now." Millions heeded.

"Just as I Am"
Charlotte Elliott

Just as I am—without one plea
But that Thy blood was shed for me
And that Thou bid'st me come to Thee—
O Lamb of God, I come!

Just as I am—and waiting not
To rid my soul of one dark blot,
To Thee, whose blood can cleanse each spot—
O Lamb of God, I come!

Just as I am—though toss'd about,
With many a conflict, many a doubt,
Fightings and fears within, without—
O Lamb of God, I come!

Just as I am—poor, wretched, blind;
Sight, riches, healing of the mind,
Yea, all I need, in Thee to find—
O Lamb of God, I come!

Just as I am—Thou wilt receive,
Wilt welcome, pardon, cleanse, relieve,
Because Thy promise I believe—
O Lamb of God, I come!

Just as I am—Thy love unknown
Has broken every barrier down;
Now to be Thine, yea, Thine alone—
O Lamb of God, I come!

Just as I am—of that free love,
The breadth, length, depth, and height to prove,
Here, for a season, then above—
O Lamb of God, I come!

INTRODUCTION

I n every generation, Christians sing their faith in lyrics that reflect their circumstances and music that mirrors their times. Like other music, Christian hymns offer a window on a culture and reveal its confidence and brokenness. Taken together over the centuries, they express the cumulative adoration, aspirations, failures, and affirmations that shape a global community of faith. A few hymns speak broadly over time and become part of the enduring-yet-ever-expanding record of repentance, yearning, testimony, and aspiration that charts an unbroken and ecumenical history of Christian devotion. Billy Graham and his associates George Beverly Shea and Cliff Barrows recognized the universal appeal and usefulness of music wedded to preaching and made it an anchor of a new and global burst of evangelical endeavor.

This book focuses briefly on Christian songs in a particular time—the twentieth century—and in a particular context, the worldwide evangelistic efforts of the Billy Graham Evangelistic Association (BGEA). Since Graham and the media revolution exploded on the scene at about the same time, Graham's music—choral, congregational, broadcast, live, recorded, new or familiar—reached an enormous public just as the pace of social, religious, political, and economic global transformation accelerated. As Graham and his team took a world stage, they brought to Christian publics everywhere unprecedented access to the same lyrics, music, singers, and sounds. Their singular coincidence of media savvy and musical message soon influenced how and what Christians (especially Protestants) sang.

I propose to examine the Graham music phenomenon and its role in the larger story of twentieth-century Christian music in several ways. Crusade music moved people differently; Graham, Shea, and Barrows affirmed repeatedly the music's power in their own lives. Graham often said that he knew of no better evangelistic tool than a gospel song well sung, and he relied on the calm inspiration of the Shea solo that routinely preceded his sermon. As one crusade pamphlet stated, Shea's solos were so well thought out and earnest that "The Gospel invitation could be extended following his solos, so clearly is the message presented."

Crusade choirs over the years routinely professed to be transformed by what they sang. They saw the music's purpose and potential through Barrows's eyes, and their responses surfaced most clearly in the letters they plastered into scrapbooks to honor Barrows and Shea. Music gave crusade crowds their one opportunity to blend their voices in common sentiment. Between 1949 and 2005, huge numbers of rank-and-file Christians participated in the Graham organization's evangelistic endeavors through music. It is estimated that more than a million people have sung in Barrows's choirs, including the record numbers at Anaheim in 1969 (10,300) and during the 1974 Rio crusade (11,000). It is thought that overall Barrows led, in person, more than 200 million attendees in congregational song, including more than 1 million in Seoul in 1973.

Guest artists relied on their musical appeal. The plaintive, pleading lines of "Just as I Am" prodded the penitent forward. Music was everywhere fulfilling its own role for different constituencies. Its diverse meanings made it abundantly useful in the crusades.

The people who selected the music and articulated principles to govern selection and performance deserve more attention than most scholars who have studied Graham provide. Graham, Barrows, and Shea brought well-honed convictions to their work. They did not devise them on the job. What principles guided selection and performance? Why? Did they evolve over time? Barrows and Shea made much of hymn stories and published several books that described the sources of popular crusade songs. What songs stood at the core of the Graham crusade experience? Why? What were their sources? As decades passed and the original, youthful team of three became old men, crusades found music a medium for cross-generational translation. Guest artists, a common feature of crusades from the outset, influenced attendance and audience response and sometimes drew criticism from Graham's most ardent supporters. How did Barrows and Shea adapt (or not) to the media revolution and the shifting musical culture it supported? What role did crusade musical choices and performance have at a critical moment of transition in church music practices? Crusade music wove its way through more than half a century of modern evangelical history, and the following chapters hardly offer a comprehensive history. Rather, they employ one set of resources that had meaning across many religious boundaries to begin to examine a tumultuous transition in Christian song.

Graham's remarkable partnership with crusade music director Barrows and soloist Shea preceded his crusades and endured unbroken long after crusading ended—until 2013, when 104-year-old George Beverly Shea died. Their friendship withstood extraordinary demands and flourished because each was secure in his own identity and all three had one vision. Journalists routinely commented that genuine humility marked the men. They seemed to observers to have one goal and to function comfortably to complement each other's efforts to achieve it.

My thesis is straightforward. In the hands of Graham, Barrows, and Shea, crusade music provides a window on an influential practice of twentieth-century Protestant song and its content. The men's reach was so enormous that simply by doing what they did (and without necessarily trying to do more) they created a sort of center (or middle-of-the-road position) for content and performance that could serve as a benchmark, at least for Protestant Christian music in transition. They were guided by principles each adopted before they joined forces, stood squarely within a tradition of revival singing that they supplemented in ways that reflected their own times, and never altered their own styles or principles. At the same time, they found ways to use crusade platforms to encourage Contemporary Christian Music and to model for congregations how to move beyond "worship wars" into a blended style of worship. They did so partly from necessity and with some personal reluctance, but they persisted and so ended their active years having mentored contemporary Christian artists and made space for new musical forms while unapologetically valuing and celebrating the songs that had shaped them since childhood.

The following pages weave biographies of people and songs and comments on culture and media in a narrative that addresses most of a century. Billy Graham is omnipresent, but he is not my primary focus. Yet he was always the first among equals in the platform team-of-three, and Barrows and Shea deferred to him and made his goals their own. Like Alexandre Dumas's Three Musketeers, the men professed to live "all for one, and one for all," and as one, they were known to hold each other accountable. Graham addressed his only public comment at his ninety-fifth birthday party in a packed-out banquet facility in Asheville, North Carolina, to Barrows, the surviving member of the original team, thanking his song leader and right-hand man for making it all possible. When Graham died, the nation paused to do him honor and remember his wide-ranging accomplishments. Graham operated in many venues beyond crusades, but his rise began in evangelistic meetings, and the Graham the world came to know would have been impossible without Barrows, Shea, and the music in which they cradled Graham's message. Their public presentation never wavered: it featured solidarity, and it is difficult to document disagreements or tensions in their relationship. The public image made much of harmony precisely because the men really did get along. The researcher can glean only the barest hints of brief discord; for example, when Shea proved the most resistant to Christian rock or when Barrows on occasion found Shea needing sensitive handling. But the men resolved any disagreements and by all accounts did so among themselves, Shea and Barrows routinely acceding to Graham because that was what each had vowed before God to do when it all began in the 1940s. Was it all perception? A chorus of global commentary over sixty years suggests not. Observers hostile and friendly said much the same thing: genuine humility and sincere consideration combined with piety molded a ministry team that really did get along. Over their six decades together, nothing seriously jeopardized their partnership and mutual regard. The three men enduringly affirmed that they shared one purpose, one calling, and one ministry that gave expression to one message within and beyond the crusades in word and song.

In so doing, they used hymns as biographies. Hymns told the crusade story of biblical truth, rendering the narrative of sin and redemption in ways that mattered in all times and places. The solid crusade foundation rested on the truths of Scripture proclaimed in sermon and song, not optional but essential and exclusive, often couched in narrative as well as in theological dogma. Like Scripture and sermon, hymns communicated the gospel as parable, prophecy, invitation, and narrative. Graham, Barrows, and Shea did their best to use hymns to tell of full salvation in all its biblical forms. Like Charles Spurgeon, they believed that preaching the gospel meant declaring the whole gospel, using every means possible. A partial proclamation was not the gospel.

Hymns as biographies of crusades may seem an unusual characterization. Yet biographies write the stories of lives—lost, redeemed, useful, reprobate, consecrated, selfish. Hymns are about missions and service, righteousness and duty, social awakening, and faithfulness. In short, they are the story of the Christian life. They tell that story, judge it, inspire it, and as Timothy Dudley-Smith said, "Tell out the greatness of the Lord." In the process of their use, hymns were transformed from individual songs arising out of varied circumstances to a particular "set" of songs that told a particular crusade story that always ended with human response to God's invitation—"I come to Thee." Other phrases captured unforgettable crusade biographical moments—"I'd rather have Jesus than anything this world affords to-day." Still others, deeply personal—"This is my story, this is my song." Or "When Jesus comes, the Tempter's power is broken" and "That on the cross, my burden gladly bearing, he bled and died to take away my sin," and "Great is thy faithfulness, Lord, unto me." Or, "The vilest offender who truly believes, that moment from Jesus a pardon receives." Or, "And can it be that I should gain an interest in the Savior's blood? Died he for me who caused his pain? For me, who him to death pursued?" And "In the cross, in the cross be my glory ever." The Graham crusades could not have had a better biography.

A SHARED PURPOSE

I am resolved no longer to linger
Charmed by the world's delight;
Things that are higher, things that are nobler,
These have allured my sight.

—"I Am Resolved,"
Palmer Hartsough, 1896

The story of the music of the Billy Graham crusades is a long, multilayered, and evolving tale. But ultimately, its essence centered upon a three-man team—William Franklin "Billy" Graham Jr., George Beverly Shea, Clifford Burton Barrows. They came from three small Christian communions—Associate Reformed Presbyterian, Wesleyan Methodist, independent Baptist. They represented three North American regions: North Carolina, Ontario (Canada), central California. They shared common roots in small-town, semirural childhoods and solid, traditional Protestant homes. Each of them had an early sense of calling to ministry. Each man resolved on his life's purpose long before they met, and so it is helpful to trace their separate paths before beginning their shared story. Shea was the first, by nearly a decade, to achieve success in the public eye and was the eldest—nine years Graham's senior and some fourteen years older than Barrows—and so we begin telling the story of the Graham crusades' music with him.

George Beverly Shea (1909–2013)

George Beverly Shea was the son of pioneer Canadian Wesleyan Methodist pastor Adam Shea and his wife, Maude Whitney. Shea's mother descended from United Empire Loyalists who had fled the American colonies during the Revolution. Her ancestors were nonetheless among the first Canadians to embrace the teachings of American Methodist circuit riders who crossed from New York into rural Ontario to evangelize pioneer settlements. Shea's father hailed from Irish immigrant stock that had arrived in Canada in the early 1800s. Adam Shea was converted in a rural revival under the preaching of female Holiness evangelists. He quickly began preaching in logging camps, was "discovered" by the American Wesleyan Church, and subsequently tagged by the Wesleyans to shepherd their expansion into Canada. By all accounts, Shea was a remarkable man whose abundant common sense, deep spiritual hunger, and willingness to learn from others made him succeed against the odds.

Their son George Beverly Shea began life on a blustery Monday, February 1, 1909, in Winchester, a thriving farming hub just off the main road linking Canada's capital, Ottawa, and the St. Lawrence River to the south. The Shea family already included two daughters, Pauline (1902) and Mary Evangeline (1906), and one son, John Whitney (1904). Adam and Maude Shea named their second son for towering figures in their lives—his maternal grandfather, George Whitney, and the popular contemporary Methodist Holiness preacher from Mississippi, Beverly Carradine (grandfather and great-grandfather of the actors John Carradine and David, Keith, and Robert Carradine). The Sheas called their new thirteen-pound arrival by his middle name, Beverly. Four siblings would follow his birth over the next decade.

Young Beverly Shea showed an early fascination for music. It began at home, where his family liked nothing better than to make music together. "Something moved my young heart deeply in those gospel hymns," Shea recalled in his old age. The language of hymns and the phrases of the King James Bible were the practical core of the heritage Adam and Maude Shea intended to pass on to their sons and daughters. At daily prayers, the family sang together, and the children memorized the hymns that warmed their parents' hearts. Each meal began with a song and prayer and concluded with the family kneeling around the table while the parents prayed aloud. For several years, the Shea children's daily morning alarm clock was their mother's voice raised in "Singing I Go," a recent (1902/1898) song by Eliza Hewitt, author of hymns such as "More about Jesus," and "When We All Get to Heaven":

> Singing I go along life's road,
> Praising the Lord, praising the Lord!
> Singing I go along life's road,
> For Jesus has lifted my load.

The stanzas brimmed with the practical advice that governed the Shea household:

> The trusting heart to Jesus clings,
> Nor any ill forebodes,
> But at the cross of Calv'ry sings
> "Praise God for lifted loads."

A beautifully crafted three-quarter-size piano stood in the sprawling Wesleyan manse. Adam Shea's wedding gift to his bride, it was the centerpiece of the Shea home until Maude Shea's death in 1971. At that piano, Maude Shea taught Beverly the basic chords. He took it from there, eventually learning to play the piano, violin, organ, trombone, and even the musical saw. Painfully shy, he refused to sing or play in public, but he found in the keyboard an outlet for his emotions, and his siblings remembered that Beverly Shea's "lonely moods" often drew him to the organ in his father's empty church sanctuary.

In 1926, the seventeen-year-old Beverly Shea devoted a month to helping at a camp meeting seventy miles away in picturesque Westport, Ontario. He did whatever he was told—setting up, working on the grounds, helping in the kitchen, ushering, publicizing the meetings. At the urging of the coevangelist, a close family friend, he sang his first solo, "He Died of a Broken Heart." The effort did not go well: his voice cracked halfway through. Persuaded to try again in a lower key the next evening, Shea succeeded and so—before a small, affirming rural Ontario crowd—unpretentiously launched what became an international solo career.

By that time his family had moved to the nation's capital, Ottawa, where Adam Shea served Sunnyside Wesleyan Church. That fall, evangelists Fred and Kittie Suffield held weeklong revival services at the church. During the

Friday night altar call, Adam Shea moved from the platform to his son's side in the last pew and said, "I think tonight might be the night, Son." As the congregation sang "Just as I Am," father and son knelt together at the front of the small sanctuary. That night, Bev Shea publicly acknowledged his parents' faith as his own, a public acknowledgment that was a rite of passage for Wesleyans. During early childhood Shea and his siblings had—in the common parlance of the day—"given their hearts to Jesus" at home, but the public profession sealed those youthful vows in the way expected in their tradition.

His parents' example inclined him toward evangelistic work, but it was clear from the start that his field would be music rather than preaching. Throughout his boyhood, his father preached in camp meetings while his mother and her parents provided musical support. Bev Shea knew from lifelong experience that music and evangelism went hand in hand. "My ultimate occupation will hover about the evangelistic field, I expect," he wrote to a friend at Houghton College in 1928 when he was nineteen, "favoring the musical side of this, God's great work."

In 1927, Shea enrolled for a year at Annesley College, a small Holiness school in Ottawa that offered biblical training and musical opportunities. Shea sang bass for the school's male quartet and developed a friendship with the quartet's tenor, Alonzo Scharfe, whose family operated a dairy farm on the edge of the city. One evening the group sang at a special service at the Bosworths' Gospel Tabernacle, where Bev Shea pointed out an attractive young woman. Scharfe identified her as his sister, Erma. Shea sought out her acquaintance, she accepted his attentions, and they began what became a seven-year courtship.

In 1928, Shea left Annesley to enroll in the newly accredited music program at the Wesleyan Church's Houghton College in upstate New York. In his spare time, Shea joined the second violins in the Houghton orchestra and provided both instrumental and vocal support for student evangelistic teams in the hamlets surrounding Houghton. While he excelled at Houghton in all things musical, enjoyed the school's social scene, and was implicated in his share of campus pranks, he showed little interest in the liberal arts education Houghton offered. In 1929, Shea withdrew to join his family at his father's new pastorate in Jersey City, New Jersey.

Once in New Jersey, the twenty-year-old Shea found employment in lower Manhattan at the Mutual of New York Insurance Company (Yankee great Lou Gehrig was one of his customers), where he earned enough to add private voice lessons to his busy schedule. He also made musical connections in the New York metropolitan area, spending hours at Calvary Baptist Church listening to distinguished organist J. Thornton Noe practice on the church's pipe organ. New friendships with Calvary Baptist musicians opened doors that helped him begin to realize his larger ambitions.

It was becoming evident that Shea's voice could be a ticket to success. Shea's voice, and his eagerness to use it at any time, began opening several doors in the emerging world of Christian broadcasting. His first forays into Christian radio had begun around 1930 when he sang live with a quartet on Erling C. Olsen's New York–based devotional program, *Bible Hour*, and on Elmo Bateman's *Gospel Hour*. The power and range of his voice were well suited to the new medium. He rose before dawn to reach radio stations in time for early morning broadcasts and then hurried on to work.

However, Shea was torn about his immediate future. He was missing Erma Scharfe (he had unsuccessfully applied for a transfer to Mutual's Ottawa offices) but knew that he did not want to spend his life in the insurance business. It was at about this time that Shea felt "the world" beckoning him to compromise the strict standards his parents upheld when he landed an audition with Ted Mack, the talent agent for *Major Bowes Amateur Hour* on New York's WHN. But this was not the way in which he had envisioned success. The lure of a career in secular entertainment or radio caused him no shortage of confusion and guilt. At a crossroads, Shea renewed his earlier vow to use his voice exclusively for gospel work. He later would often recount this decision to his public: it crystallized around the hymn that became Shea's signature song.

Shea enjoyed a close relationship with his parents, but they refrained from mentioning their concerns about Bev's interest in a secular musical career. Rather, in good Holiness fashion, they prayed and waited. Their answer came on a Saturday evening when Maude Shea clipped a poem by Rhea Miller titled "I'd Rather Have Jesus" from a religious periodical. Maude Shea glued the poem to cardboard and placed it on the piano, knowing that her son would see it there. He read it early the next morning; the words instantly soothed his mind; and he composed a tune on the spot. (Miller had already published the lyrics with her own tune, but Shea later told her that he lacked proficiency in reading the piano chords and so more easily composed his own setting.) A few hours later he accompanied himself on the reed organ in his father's church as he introduced the new hymn. It became his lifelong testimony, a fixture in his repertoire wherever he went, typically introduced with a brief testimony about its meaning in his life:

> I'd rather have Jesus than silver or gold,
> I'd rather be his than have riches untold, . . .
> I'd rather have Jesus than anything
> This world affords today.

The words had been written in 1922 in Brooktondale, New York, a town in the Finger Lakes region a few miles from Ithaca. The poem summarized how Rhea Miller, wife of a young pastor in the Church of the Nazarene, perceived her father's conversion. Martin James Ross, a grocer in Syracuse, had once been an alcoholic. His wife and friends prayed for his conversion until he experienced a life-transforming moment. He became a Baptist preacher and director of the City Rescue Mission in Binghamton before moving to Brooktondale, where he served a small Baptist congregation. His future son-in-law, Howard Miller, professed faith at a revival in Brooktondale Baptist Church, pursued his education at nearby Colgate College, and returned to Brooktondale to marry Rhea Ross. The young couple, soon joined by her parents, had their hearts "warmed" in a Nazarene revival, left the Baptist church, and planted a local congregation and campground for the Church of the Nazarene.

While walking in the family's Brooktondale fields one day in 1922, Rhea Miller pondered the consistent refrain of her father's oft-repeated testimony. Each time he spoke of his past, Ross asserted his preference for his present circumstances with the words "I'd rather have Jesus." She wrote the poem as a summary of her father's declaration of Christ's superiority to anything the world had ever offered him. Miller's text became Shea's testimony and theme song in his expanding circle of opportunity.

His new theme song came as Bev Shea had settled upon his direction in his life. His long courtship with Erma Scharfe finally led to their marriage on June 16, 1934, at Sunnyside Wesleyan Church in Ottawa. Their honeymoon took the couple to Niagara Falls, with a Sunday stopover in Buffalo, New York, to attend Churchill Tabernacle, the congregation founded by Methodist radio broadcaster Clinton Churchill. Churchill operated Buffalo's first and most powerful radio station, WKBW ("Well Known Bible Witness"). The Sheas listened eagerly to his choir and musicians, meeting pianist and composer B. D. Ackley, then Churchill's minister of music. Shea had a lifelong interest in meeting hymn writers, and both Benjamin DeForest Ackley and his brother, Alfred Henry (A. H.) Ackley, would cross his path repeatedly. The brothers had long evangelistic experience alongside Billy Sunday, and A. H. had written the beloved gospel song "He Lives." As Shea's interests expanded, he valued advice from such seasoned contemporaries.

Following their honeymoon, the newlyweds settled into an apartment back in New Jersey. Erma Shea found an opportunity to study piano with teachers affiliated with the Juilliard School, while her husband filled his free time with voice lessons, radio appearances, and solo opportunities. Later in 1934, Shea made the acquaintance of Jack Wyrtzen, a brown-eyed, black-haired bundle of energy employed at an insurance firm near Shea's office. A recently converted dance-band conductor and trombonist, Wyrtzen had big plans for youth outreach, and he immediately enlisted Shea's assistance. They and a few others began modestly with street meetings and church rallies. Combining dynamic music, energetic testimonies, and brief sermons, Wyrtzen's gatherings readily attracted young people. For musical support, Wyrtzen relied on up-tempo gospel hymns and choruses, some of them penned by other contemporary youth-oriented evangelists. In 1940, he started broadcasting his Saturday-night youth rallies and expanded the regional reach of his ministry. Shea became a part of Wyrtzen's circle and would continue to assist him for a number of years—even after Shea later moved out of the New York area.

Another young man on the move entered the Sheas' lives in the mid-1930s. Percy Bartimus Crawford had begun broadcasting the *Young People's Church of the Air* in Philadelphia in 1931, taking the title of "pastor" of this unusual radio church. In 1933, he married Ruth Duvall, a pianist whose musical stylings gave a distinctive sound to Crawford's broadcasts. That same year the Crawfords established Pinebrook Bible Conference, a campground and conference center a few miles from the Delaware River in northeastern Pennsylvania's popular Pocono Mountains. Crawford scheduled prominent fundamentalist speakers and musicians during the summer months, and George Beverly Shea quickly signed on to provide a week each year for Pinebrook's music ministry. He accepted the unsalaried duties and generally received a fifty-dollar "love offering" when he departed. Pinebrook crowds delighted in his solos and begged for recordings, which led to Shea's first record album. Produced by Jack Kapp of Decca Records (whose credits included Bing Crosby, Ethel Waters, the Dorsey Brothers, and Al Jolson), Shea was accompanied by Ruth Crawford at the organ as he rendered audience favorites, including "I'd Rather Have Jesus," "Jesus Whispers Peace," and "Lead Me Gently Home."

In 1936, citing shyness as an excuse for the five-year delay since he had appropriated her poem, Shea finally made contact with "I'd Rather Have Jesus" composer Rhea Miller; the Millers had moved from upstate New York years earlier to lead a Nazarene congregation on Chicago's South Side. Shea's tune to her lyrics had become so popular in Shea's circles that he knew something had to be done about copyright. Shea had so far refrained from singing the song on the radio, but at Pinebrook in 1936, he learned that it had been aired locally on a live broadcast in New England; meanwhile, Percy Crawford was pressuring him for permission to include the song in a new printed edition of his popular Pinebrook collection. He wrote out his tune for Miller and issued a defensive apology: "now that I see the Lord has used this combination of words and music and seems pleased to bless it, I have the needed courage to write this letter. . . . I owe you an apology."

Miller could, at that point, have made the situation difficult for Shea, but she chose simply to let him know that his delay had been inappropriate and expressed a desire to move forward on her own terms. She refused his request to pursue copyright on a joint composition and informed him of her intention to submit his tune to the musical judgment of the widely respected Church of the Nazarene hymn writer and hymnal editor Haldor Lillenas. She refused to permit Percy Crawford to publish the song despite Shea's heartwarming anecdotes of Crawford's effective use of the number as an invitation song. Shea was deeply disappointed. He had confidently informed Crawford that he was sure "the lady in Chicago" would permit publication in a songbook that promised circulation figures in the tens of thousands. Miller countered that the words set to her own tune were selling well, if not briskly, and she insisted on time to take advice.

Negotiations over the future of "I'd Rather Have Jesus" dragged on for several years. In the meantime, Shea kept up his usual schedule. He returned to Pinebrook in 1938, where the schedule featured Will Houghton, president of the Moody Bible Institute, as the speaker during Shea's week as conference musician. Houghton had the needs of Moody Bible Institute's radio station on his mind at the time and saw in Shea someone qualified to step into multiple roles at the station. The largest noncommercial religious station in the country, WMBI presented possibilities Shea had never before imagined, and Shea listened with surprise to Houghton's invitation to join the WMBI staff at a generous salary of ninety dollars per week. The position Shea was offered covered a range of duties, from auditioning staff musicians, to hosting a daily hymn broadcast called *Hymns from the Chapel*, to serving as staff announcer. Family ties in New Jersey had ended in 1935 when Shea's parents and younger siblings moved on to Adam Shea's new pastorate in central upstate New York at Willett Memorial Wesleyan Church in Syracuse. Bev Shea accepted Houghton's invitation to Chicago, and he and his wife left New Jersey in the early fall of 1938.

When Shea arrived in Chicago, he found that Moody Radio offered far more ambitious possibilities than had the strictly local broadcasts on which Shea occasionally participated in New York. *Hymns from the Chapel* gave Shea the opportunity to select the hymns he sang and to gauge listener response. He chose as his theme song "Singing I Go Along Life's Road," the family favorite from his boyhood. As he learned the ropes, he joined the singers on Houghton's popular radio program, *Let's Get Back to the Bible*. The station's musicians and preachers networked in local churches on weekends, and prominent fundamentalist visitors to Moody Bible Institute augmented regular programming. Shea had entered one of northern fundamentalism's most active circles of evangelistic preachers and forward-looking musicians.

One important friend and colleague he made was WMBI's first station manager, the talented song and chorus writer Wendell P. Loveless. Remembered as "the father of Christian radio" for his groundbreaking work at WMBI, the Wheaton, Illinois, native was also a fine musician who had penned popular gospel hymns such as "All My Sins Are Gone" and "There's Joy in Following Jesus." He was particularly known for writing dozens of upbeat, catchy, and succinct choruses that proved ideal for use in radio and youth rallies.

In his new Moody orbit, Shea also met Loveless's occasional collaborator, hymn writer Avis B. Christiansen ("Precious Hiding Place" and "Jesus, Wonderful Name"), as well as Moody Bible Institute's prolific Harry Dixon

Loes ("Blessed Redeemer," "Love Found a Way," and "Everybody Ought to Love Jesus"). The author of over two thousand hymns and choruses, Loes joined the Moody faculty in 1939 and, like Shea, became part of a circle of influential musical talent that flowed between the institute, WMBI, Moody Church, and the thriving Christian conferences at Winona Lake, Indiana. Still another Chicago colleague was William Runyan, tune writer and hymnal editor, whose credits included a then-little-known song by Thomas Obadiah Chisholm—"Great Is Thy Faithfulness." Shea also enjoyed opportunities to sing solos at the Moody Church, where he developed a warm relationship with its pastor, Harry Ironside.

Shea's new job gave him the opportunity to bring others into his own developing circle. One of his hires was Donald P. Hustad, who auditioned with Shea for a job as staff organist at WMBI and was hired on the spot. Hustad went on to a distinguished career as director of the Sacred Music Department at Moody Bible Institute and later moved to Southern Baptist Seminary in Louisville. A noted author and hymnal editor, he later served for more than six years as an organist at Billy Graham crusades during the 1960s.

Another Moody connection was musician and publisher Alfred B. Smith, who graduated from Moody Bible Institute in 1937, the year before the Sheas moved to Chicago. In 1939, Wheaton College awarded Smith a scholarship, and upon enrolling there, he met the young Billy Graham. Their shared passion for evangelism soon made them a team: during their student years they worked together in a congregation that met in the Masonic Lodge in downtown Wheaton, with Graham preaching and Smith leading music. By the late 1930s, Smith had begun self-publishing the inexpensive paperback collections of gospel hymns and choruses that became the Singspiration Series. Eventually distributed by the Grand Rapids–based Zondervan Publishing Company, the chorus books sold by the hundreds of thousands, shaping both the vocabulary and sound of congregational singing and fundamentalist broadcasting. Singspiration eventually branched out into records, and in 1947, Shea began recording for Smith's label, further building his public.

Shea remained at Moody into 1944, when he took several months of summer leave to return to New York to assist Jack Wyrtzen in what were now being called Word of Life Rallies. A decade after Wyrtzen, Shea, and others (Harry Bolback, Carlton Booth) began modestly with street preaching and Saturday-evening rallies at the Gospel Tabernacle in Times Square, the onset of World War II had brought a new urgency to Wyrtzen's efforts. New York City was alive with evangelistic opportunity, as it was the primary departure point for soldiers and airmen on their way to deployment in Europe and North Africa. Wyrtzen preached six days each week and packed the city's St. Nicholas Arena every Saturday night for a combined youth rally and radio broadcast. His annual rally at Manhattan's Madison Square Garden was tremendously successful; journalists regularly reported that twenty thousand people jammed the seventeen-thousand-seat venue, while thousands more listened outside. Shea thoroughly enjoyed the months of participating in Wyrtzen's energetic circle. He had clearly become dissatisfied at WMBI, and the time in New York offered him some needed space to consider his future without having to relinquish music evangelism.

Shea returned to Chicago in September, and by year's end had decided to resign his post at WMBI in order to host *Club Time*, a new daily hymn program sponsored by Chicago's Club Aluminum Company. Founded in 1923 with a line of "scientifically created" aluminum cookware "with tight fitting covers," Club Aluminum was headed by Herbert J. Taylor, a devout conservative Christian wanting to advertise his pots and pans while somehow spreading the gospel. Familiar with Shea from his work on WMBI, Taylor hired Shea to emcee the fifteen-minute program as well as sing hymns and gospel songs. It was on *Club Time* that Beverly Shea was transformed into *George* Beverly Shea. Convinced that audiences would be confused by hearing about a man named "Beverly," the program's advertising agency was adamant that the program host use his full name. So, *Club Time*—hosted by George Beverly Shea—debuted on the ABC Radio Network and the Armed Forces Network in September 1944.

Shea's new responsibilities on *Club Time* gave him a presence on the country's most popular weekday morning radio network. ABC advertised "listenable" programs that "naturally brightened a woman's day," and Shea's fan mail verified that his primary audience consisted of women and children. Leo Burnett, Club Aluminum's ad agency, reported in 1947 that the program provided Shea an audience of well over two and a half million individual listeners for each broadcast. Shea's contract with *Club Time* required him to promote the program by singing every Sunday morning and evening at different Chicago-area churches, one in the morning, another in the evening. His radio audience was eager to hear him in person, and attendance was strong—monitored weekly by the sponsors at Club Aluminum. He occasionally begged Club Aluminum for a Sunday off, but those weeks were few and far between. In October 1945, he offered twelve live concerts (most sponsored by churches or Youth for Christ), at which sponsors promoted the broadcast. In two months that fall, he reported an aggregate audience of thirty-four thousand.

Shea's repertoire on *Club Time* included standard hymns and old and new gospel favorites, often chosen in response to listener requests. Listeners complimented Shea's "fine voice" and called the program a bright spot amid the soap operas, jazz programs, and liquor ads that filled the airwaves. He had no dedicated secretarial help, but he and his wife sent copies of songs on request and answered letters as they could. Correspondence was generally complimentary, but the occasional listener proved impossible to please. One particularly difficult fan demanded that Shea visit her home to sing in person for a sick child. He telephoned instead, and she responded with a sharp reproof insisting that Jesus would have made time for a one-hundred-mile roundtrip, midweek visit.

Shea's frequent correspondence with his sponsors indicated his devotion to his work. He suggested improvements, convinced Club Aluminum to record a few programs so that he could listen to them critically, remarked on the absence of flyers for *Club Time* on the Club Aluminum displays in Chicago department stores, and kept a keen eye on listener feedback. During a few busy weeks, he and his wife mailed out 1,390 requested copies of the popular World War I–era hymn "God Bless Our Boys." Such added behind-the-scenes work was not in Shea's contract. Radio work consumed his time. He did what he could despite live broadcasts, concerts every weekend, and the lack of a secretary to handle correspondence. All the time, he was growing in ways that set him up for his long career as Billy Graham's soloist. He learned what he wanted in an accompanist, what kinds of amplification he preferred, what style podium suited him, what songs people loved, and how best to publicize his efforts.

Perhaps most importantly for the future, *Club Time* expanded Shea's understanding of the church: his responsibilities took this son of a Wesleyan Methodist manse into congregations of all denominations, and to his initial surprise, he found like-minded people of faith everywhere. He worked directly with Club Aluminum's president, Herbert J. Taylor, who supported many different evangelistic endeavors, and also came to know and admire Taylor's friend Robert Walker, an emerging journalist who in the future would often cover Graham and his team.

During these years in Chicago, Shea at last had an opportunity to meet Rhea and Howard Miller. With Miller's permission, he now regularly used "I'd Rather Have Jesus" in his radio solo repertoire. He had many requests for a copy of the hymn, but his version was still not copyrighted and an arrangement was long overdue. The Millers now agreed to help Shea publish her words to his tune. They filed for joint copyright and agreed to strict limitations on copyright permissions, routinely refusing requests for the song to appear in hymnals intended for North American use. To the delight of Shea's radio audiences, they created a hymnal-sized steel plate of words and four-part harmony that enabled printing and distribution. Moody Press marketed the sheet music for fifteen cents (two for a quarter), and Shea distributed autographed copies on request. During the 1940s, more than eight thousand copies of the song circulated as sheet music. Miller and Shea permitted publication—in translation—only in hymnals not intended for circulation in the United States. Royalties from "I'd Rather Have Jesus" funded several hospitals and schools in Africa through Church of the Nazarene missions.

Radio work in Chicago positioned Bev Shea for a strategic role in the stirrings within fundamentalism that would soon shape the modern evangelical movement. Focused on youth, immersed in new media, and eager to use lively music to capture the attention of their generation, emerging young leaders confirmed Shea in his decision to use his voice for evangelism. Shea's familiarity with Jack Wyrtzen's accomplishments and Percy Crawford's success convinced him that the Chicago area needed its own dose of strategic youth evangelism. To lead the effort he set his sights on Torrey Johnson, the young founder and pastor of Chicago's Midwest Bible Church, and pursued him for months until he agreed to organize a series of youth rallies with the help of Johnson's brother-in-law and copastor, future Christian broadcaster Robert A. Cook. "God used Beverly Shea," Torrey Johnson acknowledged when he recounted the Youth for Christ story. This stunningly successful initiative adopted a motto that captured the intent of its sponsors: "Geared to the times; anchored to the Rock."

Billy Graham (1918–2018)

Billy Graham looms over the story of mid-twentieth-century evangelical music in a surprising way. Graham could not sing (Shea once quipped that Graham suffered from "the malady of no melody"), and he delegated most musical decisions to Barrows and Shea, but he created the setting that made their work matter. Like his tone-deaf predecessor D. L. Moody, Graham recognized the importance of singing in evangelistic endeavors: he saw music and the spoken word as a seamless whole in the pursuit of one objective—an individual decision.

Born on Thursday, November 7, 1918, on a dairy farm near Charlotte, North Carolina, Graham was the first child of Morrow Coffey and William Franklin Graham Sr. Farm chores, school, church, and baseball occupied his childhood years. He memorized the Westminster Shorter Catechism, regularly worshiped with his family at an Associate Reformed Presbyterian church, and considered himself a Christian until he met Mordecai Ham, a Kentucky-born Baptist evangelist who counted among his forebears eight generations of Baptist preachers. Since 1901, Ham had been evangelizing the South. An outspoken temperance advocate with a political—and sometimes racist—edge to his message, Ham nevertheless gained a reputation as a biblical and direct preacher. One admirer explained: "He exalts Christ and fights sin with all his might. There is no middle ground in his campaigns."

In the fall of 1934, Ham and his song leader, William J. Ramsay, opened a campaign at a revival tabernacle in Charlotte. Graham's parents attended, but their sixteen-year-old teenaged son wanted nothing to do with evangelists. Nearly a month passed before he agreed to go, drawn more by the opportunity to drive a friend's truck to the tabernacle than by any spiritual longing. When Ham rose to preach, though, everything changed. Graham recalled sitting spellbound through that first sermon, and he began attending nightly. Baptized, catechized, and confirmed in the Associate Reformed Presbyterian Church, Graham did not think of himself as a sinner until Ham's sermons made him see himself in a new light. One memorable evening in November 1934 Graham made his decision. Several hundred people moved forward as Ramsay led the crowd in "Just as I Am." Penitents kept coming, so Ramsay segued into the somber pleading of "Almost Persuaded." Graham finally yielded during the last stanza of the invitation music. A family friend moved behind him, explained what he had to do to receive Christ, and prayed with him. Graham checked "recommitment" on the card he completed and regarded that evening as the moment he intentionally appropriated the Christian nurture and training that had always enveloped his life.

Upon graduating from high school in 1936, Graham enrolled at Bob Jones College, then located in Cleveland, Tennessee. Jones, a seasoned Methodist evangelist and early religious broadcaster, opened his fundamentalist school in Florida in 1927 and moved it to Tennessee in 1933. Though students admired "Dr. Bob" personally, some bristled under the stern rules that guided his college. Graham found both classroom learning and social expectations confining. He wanted to study in an environment that welcomed questions rather than parroted Jones's views. Graham recalled later that each dorm room featured a plaque that read "Griping Not Tolerated!" When he sought an interview with Jones, Graham learned that the evangelist meant what he said. Jones informed him that he was a failure and was likely to continue as such.

Graham withdrew after one semester and transferred to Florida Bible Institute (FBI) in Tampa, a school run by a Christian and Missionary Alliance evangelist from North Carolina. There he yielded to his call to the ministry and began preaching at the Tampa Gospel Tabernacle and at evangelistic campaigns in neighboring towns. Even in these earliest meetings, music played a major role in Graham's efforts. His first revivals not only touted his preaching but also played up the presence of his song leader, one Ponzi Pennington. Graham's first radio appearance on a Florida station largely used his preaching to fill in the gaps between musical numbers.

Baptized by immersion in 1938, Graham was ordained to ministry in the Southern Baptist Convention in February 1939. He graduated from FBI in 1940 and enrolled that fall at Wheaton College in the western suburbs of Chicago, where his studies in anthropology did not deter him from continuing his evangelism. In 1941, Graham became pastor of United Gospel Tabernacle, a congregation in downtown Wheaton, but he still made time to conduct evangelistic services in neighboring areas. Just before graduating from Wheaton, Graham accepted the pastorate of the Western Springs Baptist Church (also known as the Village Church). In August 1943 he traveled to North Carolina to marry a fellow Wheaton student, Ruth McCue Bell, the daughter of missionaries to China who had settled in the Presbyterian retreat center at Montreat in the North Carolina mountains. The new-lyweds returned to a home in Western Springs, and their church, meeting in a basement auditorium, began to grow.

As Graham headed into the fall of 1943 and tackled the challenges of pastoring a church, he also assumed responsibility for a radio broadcast that came with the job. *Songs in the Night* was a live forty-five-minute Sunday evening (10:15–11:00) program carried over WCFL (1000 AM—"Chicago's Voice of Labor") that had only begun the previous June. Graham had token financial backing from the congregation for the program and knew that he had to grow his listener base to make the ministry self-sustaining. Believing he needed a "marquee name" to lend a hand with music, Graham honed in on George Beverly Shea as the man who could help make *Songs in the Night* a spiritual and financial success. Graham had never met Shea, but he knew his career as a radio personality and recording artist was thriving. In Graham's world, Shea was a celebrity—in later years he and Ruth liked to recall how they had seen him on their first date when they attended the same performance of *Messiah*. Just as important for Graham, however, was that he liked how and what Shea sang. Shea possessed a clear sense of vocation and strong convictions about using his voice to *sing a message*. The Ontario native was already known for his ability to convey deep religious conviction with his resonant bass-baritone voice, impeccable diction, and sensitive phrasing. Additionally, despite his years in radio and in the public eye as a singer, Shea remained a humble man, eschewing mannerisms that suggested anything theatrical.

So it was that on a fall day Graham made his way down to the Moody Bible Institute, found WMBI's offices, strode past the secretarial pool, and walked unannounced into Shea's office. The young preacher presented his situation and laid out his offer. Much to Graham's relief and, perhaps, to his surprise, Shea agreed to come onboard. Graham gratefully gushed that the music on *Songs in the Night* would equal the best anywhere. He was less certain, he said, about the preaching.

The first broadcast of the reconfigured program and new partnership aired on January 2, 1944. As it evolved, the program featured announcer Vincent Hogren, Shea, and the Village Church choir and organist, interspersed with brief meditations from Graham. The model for this easy-listening Sunday night format had been created years earlier on Chicago's airwaves by evangelist and broadcaster Paul Rader, who envisioned it as a meditative, low-key way to end the Lord's Day. Shea's involvement immediately attracted a late-night congregation at the church as well as over the airwaves. Radio mail and Graham's personal engagements soon required the attention of two full-time secretaries.

Within weeks, Graham knew he had made the right choice, as the program paid its way. Audience response to *Songs in the Night* and the Graham/Shea team supported Graham's belief that Shea's musical involvement would command a wide listenership: "I especially enjoy Beverly Shea's singing. I listen to him every afternoon on his Club Aluminum program. . . . It is so wonderful to hear someone with such unusual talent dedicating this talent to the Lord in this age of so much worldly entertainment." Another listener expressed a common sentiment about Shea's singing: "He has the most beautiful voice I've ever heard. It seems it is just filled with the Holy Spirit. When he sings, it seems like the Holy Spirit speaks." Listeners often requested particular songs: "I hope Mr. Shea can sing soon and often 'I'd Rather Have Jesus than Anything.' It is the most beautiful hymn written, probably because it is so true."

As Shea partnered with Graham in other Village Church endeavors, the two developed a warm friendship. He sang regularly for a series of Graham's men's breakfasts that attracted some 250 men and otherwise made himself available to his blossoming endeavors. Graham relied on Shea so much that he called him his "assistant pastor." In fact, Shea preached several times in Graham's absences and told Graham that the congregation was finding out that he was "not so good at it." In 1944, the Grahams found the Sheas a home near their own. Shea quipped that he could afford his Chicago apartment at $47.50 per month, but the house listed for $8,900. A friend loaned $2,500, and the Grahams arranged the remaining financing that made it possible for the Sheas to move to the suburbs. The two couples cemented a lifelong friendship.

In the fall of 1944 Graham unexpectedly learned that his long-simmering application to become a military chaplain had been approved. Resigning his position at the Village Church to head to Harvard Divinity School for his chaplaincy training course, Graham gave Shea full charge of *Songs in the Night*, and he would remain with the broadcast until 1951. (For his part, Graham came down with a serious case of the mumps before he could begin his training. He was forced to spend months recuperating in North Carolina and resigned his commission before moving on to other endeavors.)

Now that Graham was freed up for new endeavors, an earlier connection he had made back in the Chicago area began to bear fruit. At the beginning of his Western Springs pastorate, Graham had become friends with Midwest Bible Church pastor and radio broadcaster Torrey Johnson, a fellow alum of Wheaton College (class of 1930). The two first met in 1943 when Johnson wanted Graham to take over *Songs in the Night*. But their relationship quickly grew thanks, in part, to Shea's earlier connections to Johnson.

In the spring of 1944, Johnson began to move on the vision for a youth rally ministry that Shea had encouraged him to embrace. Johnson enlisted some of his well-connected church members to find a venue for the rallies and was able to rent out Chicago's historic Orchestra Hall for the duration of the Chicago Symphony Orchestra's summer break. Johnson convinced Graham to speak at the inaugural rally, and the organizers waited in suspense to see if anyone would attend. The first rally filled Orchestra Hall on May 27, and weekly rallies continued through the summer with different speakers and novel gimmicks to interest a steady succession of overflow crowds. Some Saturday evenings, the hall emptied, only to refill immediately with thousands who could not gain entrance to the first event. When summer ended with a final rally on October 21 that drew thirty thousand people to the Chicago Stadium, the Saturday evening events continued in the commodious auditorium of Moody Memorial Church.

By August 1944, a group of leaders engaged in citywide youth rallies from across the country gathered at Winona Lake, Indiana (then a popular fundamentalist conference center), to create a temporary organization for their mutual benefit and support. Johnson recruited Graham as the group's first full-time evangelist. By 1945, Youth for Christ (YFC) had become a permanent national entity. Shea had helped birth the organization; Johnson was chosen as its first president; and Graham became its first official voice. The organizers prepared a constitution that committed the founders to encouraging youth evangelism and emphasizing "radiant, victorious Christian living." Its most ambitious early program was a Memorial Day rally at Chicago's Soldier Field on May 30, 1945. Billed as "The Greatest Youth Gathering in History," the extravaganza featured a long roster of popular fundamentalists, from Charles E. Fuller of *Old-Fashioned Revival Hour* fame to track star Gil Dodds, the "Flying Parson," who ran two laps around the field and offered a testimony. Patriotic songs and hymns punctuated a four-hour program. Four hundred uniformed army nurses walked the field in cross formation; color guards marched; Navy Lt. Robert Evans made an appeal for war bonds. Brief talks by popular speakers, missionary pageants, and abundant music filled the hours. Barely a year after organizers wondered if anyone would attend a youth rally at Orchestra Hall, YFC packed out Chicago's mammoth Soldier Field with a crowd of seventy-five thousand.

Graham's June 1945 summer travels for YFC included a few meetings at the Ben Lippen (Mountain of Trust) Conference back in North Carolina. An extensive property near Asheville owned by Columbia Bible College, the venue hosted popular meetings and conferences, and Graham was scheduled for a series of services. One night he discovered that neither song leader nor accompanist was in attendance. Someone told him that a musical couple on their honeymoon sat in the audience. He enlisted their help, brushed off a comment about their inexperience with the words "beggars can't be choosers," and strode to the platform as Billie Barrows took her place at the piano and twenty-two-year-old Cliff Barrows hurried to their car for his trombone. And so Billy Graham met Cliff Barrows.

Clifford Burton Barrows (1923–2016)

Born on April 6, 1923, in Ceres, California, near Modesto in the San Joaquin Valley, Cliff Barrows was the first child of Charles Tillson Barrows, a farmer and a buyer for the Sacramento-based Thornton Cannery, and Harriet Maurine Griggs. His childhood centered around home, church, school, and an endless round of chores on the family farm. The Barrows men enjoyed working with their hands. Charles Barrows built the family home and added on to it as his family grew. Cliff Barrows learned from his father practical skills that served him well in his life's work, and he cherished memories of father-son fishing trips for salmon and trout.

Barrows's mother came from a music-loving family of instrumentalists and vocalists. While Charles appreciated music, his son liked to say he "could not carry a tune in a bucket, no matter how big the bucket." Nonetheless, he sang—and played the mandolin and banjo. Music filled the Barrows home as Cliff and his sisters formed a trio that performed locally. The family featured prominently in every program at the Ceres

Baptist Church, singing, reciting, playing instrumental solos, or performing with the church orchestra (where Harriet played the violin and Charles
strummed his mandolin).

The Baptist church was the oldest and largest congregation in Ceres, a
town of one thousand. By the time Cliff was born in 1923, the roster listed
more than two hundred members. First Baptist and three other churches
(Congregational, Methodist, and Christian) anchored the social life of
the community. Glad Tidings Mission, a small Pentecostal congregation
planted by graduates of Glad Tidings Bible Institute in San Francisco, was
a recent arrival. While Charles and his immediate family and in-laws were
firmly anchored at First Baptist, his mother and siblings attended the Pentecostal mission. Cliff's aunt, Laura Barrows, graduated from Glad Tidings
Bible Institute and functioned locally for several years as a Pentecostal
pulpit supply and evangelist.

The Barrows children did well in school. Their names appeared regularly
on the honor roll and among the participants in school programs and PTA
entertainments. At Ceres High School, Cliff (class of '40) was athletic and popular, participating in swimming, basketball, baseball, soccer, and track, and
winning the Stanislaus County men's tennis championship. As leader of the
school's Christian club, the King's Messengers, Barrows's religious scruples
led him to refuse to play his trombone for school dances. However, he relished
other musical opportunities and had his first experience conducting after his
band instructor asked him to take over during the teacher's absence.

During Cliff's youth, a gifted roster of pastors led Ceres First Baptist
Church. Van Dyke Todd, a pioneer Baptist preacher in Texas and California, devoted himself particularly to evangelism and church planting. Pastors Carl Dearfelt and Paul Jackson followed him and focused on enlisting
the congregation's young people for future ministry. In the same years that
the fundamentalist-modernist controversy unsettled many Baptist congregations across the United States and Baptist conventions split amid harsh
recriminations, the Ceres church did not splinter but, rather, following
the old paths as a matter of course, associated with others who did the
same. The congregation joined the Baptist Bible Union in the late 1920s,
the forerunner of the conservative General Association of Regular Baptists
(the GARBC) formed in the 1930s. Barrows grew up in a congregation that
affirmed the inspiration of Scripture and the necessity of a new birth.

One Sunday in 1934, following a sermon on the classic invitation text John 3:16, Cliff stepped forward from the third row during the closing hymn to profess faith. As he put it, "I gave my hand to the preacher and my heart to the Savior." In the next few years, he began taking a larger place in the congregation, leading the singing on Sunday nights, playing his trombone, and learning how to motivate others to sing. He remembered for his entire life a lesson his nonmusical father taught him during the short ride home after the teenager led a Sunday evening hymn sing: lead by encouraging rather than by scolding. He recalled his favorite songs from these years: Priscilla Owens's "Jesus Saves" and Leila Morris's "Jesus Is Coming to Earth Again." His sister was a fine pianist, while his aunt, Helen Griggs (composer of the popular chorus "Gone, Gone, Gone, Gone" ["Gone, gone, gone, gone, yes my sins are gone"]), had wider musical experience and became a trusted mentor who taught him how to emphasize particular phrases while leading congregational singing. He followed his mother's advice (and demonstrated a prodigious capacity for memory) in memorizing the 352 *selections* in First Baptist's hymnal, *Tabernacle Hymns #3*. Tabernacle Publishing Company billed their hymnals as a "bouquet of splendid songs" that sang "the great Fundamentals of the Faith," and the series had a wide reach. It had firm editorial ties to musicians from the Moody Bible Institute and to Chicago-based evangelist (and former pastor of Moody Church) Paul Rader, who made sure that it included "a generous number" of "deeper life" as well as evangelistic selections. Barrows often remarked that those hymns "really taught me the Word of God. I learned the truths of the Word of God as interpreted through *Tabernacle Hymns #3*. I learned about the blood. I learned about the Holy Spirit. I learned about missions. I learned about the gospel, and I knew every page in the book." Convinced that music "carried the written Word to a deeper dimension in the mind and heart," Barrows did not stop with *Tabernacle Hymns #3* but diligently continued to expand his knowledge of hymns and their authors.

Barrows aspired to be a physician and planned to study at the University of California. He had his parents' consent and an aunt's promise to pay his tuition. Then in 1937, Barrows attended a Bible conference at the Mt. Hermon Christian Conference Grounds, where, under the preaching of Charles Richard "Dick" Hillis, missionary to China, and his brother, India missionary Don Hillis, the young teenager sensed a call to ministry.

He now joined a group of more than twenty young men in his church who professed a similar calling.

One Sunday in 1939, an impressive young visitor filled the pulpit at First Baptist. When Charles Barrows learned that the young preacher had taken his training at Bob Jones College, he told his son that he would now pay for college only if Cliff enrolled at Bob Jones, a school about which the family knew nothing. Young Cliff was intent enough on entering Christian ministry that he agreed with his father's decision.

In the fall of 1940, Cliff made the long rail journey from Ceres to Cleveland, Tennessee. He soon gained the notice of the school's founder, the legendary southern evangelist Bob Jones Sr., who apparently saw his potential and from the start numbered Barrows among his select "preacher boys." The Bob Jones College theme for Barrows's freshman year was "Victory." The school newspaper, the *Conqueror*, explained that "victory" meant "victory through Christ over sin and self." In mid-February, a revival broke out that saw students turning chapel seats into "old-time mourners' benches." Such was Barrows's introduction to Bob Jones, a place where compulsory daily chapels (including Saturdays) and nightly dorm prayer meetings cultivated any flickering flame of spiritual hunger and battled any impulse toward nonconformity. Also, Bob Jones College advertised itself as the only college in the United States that offered voice, piano, speech, and pipe organ instruction at no additional expense. Tuition, room, and board cost a modest $432, and when Barrows enrolled, the eight-year-old college registered just over five hundred students. Four-year majors (BA) were limited to music, speech, and religion, but the sacred music program included Bible training and a class in radio work. Barrows enrolled just as the school began to thrive. The student body grew dramatically during Barrows's college years, doubling in size by the time he graduated.

As the raw Billy Graham had discovered a few years earlier, student life was strictly controlled. On Sundays, all students worshiped together—Sunday school, followed by morning worship, followed by four o'clock vespers. Young people's societies affiliated with national organizations—Christian Endeavor, the Methodists' Epworth League, the Baptist Young People's Union—held services following vespers. Barrows was vice president of the Baptist Young People's Union, and his sister Mary Jean (who followed her brother to Bob Jones in 1942) was its pianist. After this full day of required activities, the administration encouraged students to attend the evening service at a church of their denomination (from an approved list, of course) in Cleveland. Seven times each week, students and faculty affirmed in unison the college creed—the inspiration of Scripture, creation of humankind by direct act of God, the incarnation, the virgin birth, vicarious atonement and bodily resurrection of Christ, the new birth, the gift of eternal life. Bob Jones Sr. mandated what he could to discourage deviation. All of this had been too much for Billy Graham, but Barrows thrived at the school from the start.

At Bob Jones, Barrows met Wilma (Billie) Newell, a Baptist pastor's daughter from Freeport, Illinois, who had a rich contralto voice and played the piano, organ, and vibraharp. She was two years behind him in her studies and had been Barrows's first roommate's "best girl." When the roommate graduated, he told Barrows he was leaving him a few books and Billie Newell. Barrows seized the moment and won Billie Newell's affection. He graduated in 1944 in a class of sixty-two after a full week of festivities and four years of active student life: vice president, freshman class; president, sophomore class; officer of the William Jennings Bryan Society (a men's social group/literary society under the motto In All Things Christ), the Baptist Young People's Union, the Pan-Hellenic Society, the Classic Players, the male quartet. He played for the nearby fundamentalist Bryan College's soccer team, served on the yearbook staff, and was listed in *Who's Who in American Universities and Colleges*. The first graduate of Bob Jones's sacred music concentration, Barrows left the school with a strong record of community involvement and the good will of the doughty Bob Jones himself.

The only fly in the ointment as he moved on was a less-than-satisfactory arrangement for the immediate future. Bob Jones College had strict rules about dating: couples could meet on campus only at specified hours in a particular room in the presence of a chaperone. Barrows broke a college rule when he went down on one knee in that room and asked Wilma Newell for her hand in marriage. Students were not permitted to marry, but he was about to graduate. Newell's father agreed to the marriage but stipulated that Barrows would have to pay for his wife's remaining college education. Barrows asked Bob Jones for permission to return for additional studies, but Jones turned him down. A disappointed Barrows journeyed home for his ordination at Ceres Baptist Church and then accepted the post of assistant pastor at Temple Baptist Church in St. Paul, Minnesota, while his fiancée completed her junior year. The young couple married on June 22, 1945.

The Barrows met Billy Graham during their brief honeymoon that June. On a shoestring budget, they took a room in a private home in Asheville, and their host volunteered the couple to fill in for an absent pianist and song leader during Graham's youth service at the nearby Ben Lippen Conference Center. And so a lifetime of friendship and partnership began around music. During the next year, Billie Barrows completed her final year of studies while Cliff Barrows honed his skills leading music for YFC rallies at a salary of $225 per month.

Dubbed "Wheel" Barrows by young admirers in YFC, Barrows was just twenty-two when a reporter introduced him in *Power Magazine* as "a reasonable facsimile of a guy a maiden might dream about" who, two minutes after he took the platform, had everyone singing, "even the photographers, because making people sing and like it [was] Cliff Barrows' specialty!" Barrows told his young YFC admirers, "I got my idea from cheerleaders. I believe if a cheer leader can put all he's got into a cheer, a song leader for the Lord ought to exert himself enough to wake up a congregation to sing with joy and enthusiasm." His early approach? "I just open my mouth and let my hands fly." "He goes into action with the vigor of a prize fighter and the grace of a ballet dancer," a Boston reporter once observed. "A human dynamo," another journalist labeled him. "His energy is something to watch. He conducts not only with his arms and his head, but with his whole body."

In time, YFC rallies and events brought Barrows to Shea's attention. Each remained busy cultivating connections that unbeknownst to them would enhance their common future endeavors even as circumstances and mutual esteem in the pulsating world of youth evangelism drew them closer together. Surrounded by opportunities and talent, it was unclear who, if anyone, in YFC circles would emerge from the talented group as a premier evangelist. In 1946 and 1947, a path forward for Graham, Barrows, and Shea as a ministry unit had begun taking shape: gradually but persistently, their shared purpose evolved into a particular shared calling.

CALLED TOGETHER

Take the task he gives you gladly;
Let his work your treasure be.
Answer quickly when he calls you,
"Here am I. Send me! Send me!"

—"Hark, the Voice of Jesus Calling,"
Daniel March, 1868

A s we have seen, Billy Graham, Cliff Barrows, and George Beverly Shea each had a clear sense of calling to ministry long before they met. It is unlikely that any of them envisioned how expansive their ministry would ultimately be—much less what shape it might finally take. But in the postwar years, their partnership in ministry would begin to slowly unfold through a set of circumstances that coincided with Billy Graham's pursuit of his call.

In March and April of 1946, Youth for Christ (YFC) commissioned a team of leaders to take their message to Europe. Amid the grim backdrop of postwar dislocation, rationing, and devastation, Graham, his Canadian buddy Charles Templeton, and pianist Stratton Shufelt accompanied YFC president Torrey Johnson to England, Scotland, Northern Ireland, Sweden, Norway, the Netherlands, Denmark, and France. Moody Church pastor Harry Ironside led a farewell service on March 17 that drew more than four thousand well-wishers. The next day, a thousand of these YFC faithful reassembled at the Chicago Municipal Airport to give the men a rousing send-off.

Upon arrival in Europe, the group split up to cover more territory, with Graham and Templeton spending three busy weeks in Great Britain prior to three additional weeks in the Netherlands, Belgium, Denmark, and France. Everywhere they attracted capacity crowds, three—and even four—times a day. Graham remembered the people as "starved for hope and hungry for God." As they traveled, the YFC team built relationships with local evangelical leaders who urged them to return. Deeply moved by what he saw—churches in ruins, food and commodities in short supply, and a precipitous decline in church attendance (a trend compounded by many ruined church buildings)—Graham sensed his future path unfolding before him. Johnson, however, brought him up short with two observations: evangelism was expensive, and he would have to raise his support himself.

Graham returned home to a busy schedule of youth rallies that, within weeks, took him to both coasts and to Canada. The burden he felt for Europe persisted, however, and in the fall of 1946 he shared it with the young song leader Cliff Barrows. Graham liked what he had seen of Cliff's and Billie Barrows's (Billie had graduated from Bob Jones College in June) ability and character as their paths had crossed in YFC work. He soon asked the Barrowses if they would accompany him to Britain for several months of meetings along with prolonged times of prayer to consider their futures in ministry. They accepted Graham's invitation, with Cliff Barrows joining Graham in agreeing to receive just half of their already meager YFC salaries while abroad. They did not have a clear idea of how long they would be gone, but they intended to spend at least the winter of 1946–1947 in Europe, where heating was scarce, buildings were in ruins, food was rationed, and hundreds of thousands of prisoners of war and displaced persons were still being repatriated. Ruth Graham (who stayed home with the Grahams' first child) promised to join them for a few weeks in December. Billy Graham had a straightforward plan for the new team: Ruth would pray, Billy preach, Cliff lead the music, and Billie play the piano. The next months would shape the foundational principles of all that followed, especially in the vision and philosophy for the crusades to come.

Graham and the Barrows did not simply pick up and depart. They guaranteed for themselves the prayers of thousands of supporters by undertaking a grueling farewell tour of YFC rallies that concluded at Chicago's Moody Church on Sunday evening, October 6, 1946. Pastor Harry Ironside was a good friend of YFC, with a particularly warm spot in his heart for the young Graham and Barrows. A photo of that memorable service shows the men kneeling before Ironside, Graham prostrate, as Ironside laid his hands on them in prayer at the front of his packed-out sanctuary. Early in October, they sailed from New York for Southampton, England, where local supporters met them. They conducted their first services in Southampton's Methodist Central Hall. Barrows brought his trombone to help him lead the singing. As they made their way across Britain, they lodged in homes, run-down hotels, and sparsely appointed rentals, freezing in unheated rooms (sometimes sleeping fully dressed, overcoats on, and still shivering) and sharing the meager rationed fare of their hosts. The British press reported that the response was unexpectedly enthusiastic; thousands flocked to the meetings, far exceeding the crowds of any other evangelists since the pre–World War I tours of Reuben A. Torrey and Charles Alexander. Just before the start of mid-February 1947 meetings in London, Graham wrote to his parents convinced that thousands had been converted.

Between engagements, Graham and Barrows studied past revivals, made connections with British evangelicals, and gained a larger sense of the spiritual and physical needs of postwar Europe. Their services brought encouraging results, especially in Belfast, where a few thousand had to be turned away nightly from a large hall crowded with thousands more. A visit to the sites associated with the Welsh revival thrilled Barrows, who had never heard anything like Welsh religious song. Contacts with emerging young British preachers like Stephen Olford and Alan Redpath deepened the Americans' grasp of the times and molded their vision for the future. Still in the throes of a recent life-transforming experience, Olford eagerly shared his convictions about "the fullness of the Holy Spirit" and the need for believers to submit "daily and hourly to the sovereignty of Christ and the authority of the word." He, Graham, and Barrows prayed together for hours until they believed they had "broken through" to a deeper experience of Ephesians 5:18: "Be filled with the Spirit." Olford, Barrows recalled, "laid on our hearts what God could do." Years later, Graham cited Olford as the greatest influence on his early ministry.

The spiritual insights that Graham and Barrows absorbed from Olford drew heavily on what was known in Britain as Keswick teaching. Since 1875, annual conventions in Keswick (in the picturesque Lake District of northwest England) attracted Protestants who believed that the Spirit-filled life was in reality what Olford called "normal Christian living." In Britain, Barrows and Graham studied the roots of this piety. They mined the resources of every nearby public and private library. At ninety years of age, Barrows still vividly recalled hours among the shelves at Foyle's Bookstore and combing secondhand bookshop inventories for titles related to revival. They read Puritans like John Owen and Thomas Watson; Keswick speakers like Handley Moule, J. C. Ryle, and G. Campbell Morgan; American authors such as A. J. Gordon and A. T. Pierson, and they pored over accounts of the 1904-1905 Welsh Revival. They examined records of famous evangelistic partnerships like that between the American team of D. L. Moody and Ira Sankey to learn how the men structured prolonged ministry in one place and how they related to local congregations.

Graham and Barrows came away from their reading with a particularly deep admiration for Moody and Sankey that influenced much of what would come in the years ahead. They admired the way in which the two men had developed a working relationship that flourished separately and together. Wherever they went, the duo took Jeremiah 32:17 as their keynote: "Nothing is too hard for [God]." They prayed over those words daily and returned to them in every difficulty. Sankey's use of music to reinforce Moody's preaching and both men's earnest approach to every service stood in contrast to the gimmicks some evangelists used to warm their audiences. Moody and Sankey worked with and through local congregations and encouraged purpose-driven, cooperative evangelistic endeavors like the Student Volunteer Movement, the YMCA, and other parachurch organizations. Scrupulous about financial accountability, they entrusted all their considerable hymnal royalties to a lay committee that distributed the funds to Christian schools. The pair ignored denominational particularities and developing theological controversies and made the familiar benchmarks of nineteenth-century American evangelicalism their central message: Bible-based faith and "know-so" conversions explained in folksy sermons, gospel songs, and standard hymns. The message and its setting drew penitents by the thousands, and Moody stood ready to put all of them to work.

British reporters marveled at Sankey's ability to make gospel songs "talk" to "the man in the street," who, if he failed to sing the verses, would chime in on the refrain. Gospel songs disarmed critics by their "manifest adaptation to an end": stirring a crowd. The point was not to replace beloved traditional hymns and psalms but, rather, to accomplish an immediate purpose. With that understood, most people readily acquiesced to the less formal music. Denomination mattered far less than the job at hand: Moody-Sankey-style Christianity made room for people who differed on many points as long as they held to a common core. As a result, nondenominational endeavors flourished, and lay leadership blossomed.

Two generations later, Graham and Barrows found inspiration and direction in the Moody-Sankey model. It suited their passion for cooperative evangelism while remaining firmly anchored in the Bible. Moody and Sankey's approach to gospel singing shaped Barrows and Graham, too. The most obvious difference was Sankey's customary place at the organ rather than the podium. Barrows had no keyboard training and would rely on accomplished accompanists, freeing himself to conduct the choir and lead the congregation. But with regard to the principles that governed the selection and performance of crusade music, Barrows stood squarely with Sankey.

When British reporters searched for an explanation of the Moody-Sankey appeal, they often started with the music. "Words of songs are strange and new, there is such earnestness about the singer, that insensibly all who go are affected, and many who do not care for the preaching express themselves astonished at the singing," reporters noticed. "Sankey's voice is uncultivated, yet his charms are great. Services have greatest order and good feeling, and nothing that can annoy." Sankey's most frequent solos became instant favorites: "The Great Physician Now Is Near"; "Sweet Hour of Prayer"; "Safe in the Arms of Jesus"; "Softly and Tenderly Jesus Is Calling"; and "The Ninety and Nine" ("There were ninety-and-nine that safely lay in the shelter of the fold"). Sankey's British admirers admitted that the Americans' songs did not approach the standards set by the acknowledged giants of English hymnody—William Cowper, John Keble, or Charles Wesley—yet they became general favorites on their home turf. "Thousands who never cared for hymns before find pleasure in them now," marveled observers. Of the two men, the *Christian Advocate* commented in 1876, "each so supplemented the other as to make it difficult to distinguish between them as to usefulness in their united work."

Barrows's readings of appreciative British authors who wrote while the glow of the Moody-Sankey meetings lingered reinforced his own instincts about the evangelistic possibilities of gospel singing. Contemporaries remarked that Sankey sang "with the conviction that souls received Jesus between one note and the next" and that his singing "threw the Lord's net" around an audience. They concurred that Sankey's music was "a great help" to the preaching because he had "power to send his voice into the soul," an ability "higher than art that captivated when art was powerless." One journalist pointed out in 1876 that Sankey was far more than a "mere choir leader." "Suppress the singing," he continued, "and you remove fully one half of the power" of the meetings. "Mr. Sankey is as truly an evangelist as his companion who does nearly all the speaking." Others concurred: "Such grace and power have characterized his singing, and such devotion and winning words his addresses and prayers in revival services that quite as much to him as to his justly esteemed associate is to be ascribed the success of the work in which both are engaged."

Barrows resonated with Sankey's caution that, while training was important, one had to be careful that "all the soul" was not "trained out" of a gospel singer, leaving singing merely an exhibition. "He must have the Gospel in his heart," Sankey insisted, "and desire to sing it out clearly and unmistakably with a plain enunciation of the words." Sankey always insisted that he avoided using music for entertainment. Even though, like many conservative Protestants, Sankey found no place for entertainment in a setting that confronted people with the choice between heaven or hell, participants certainly found his music enjoyable, if not entertaining. "I take my mission seriously," he said, but "there is no reason why we should not have meetings full of song and story, yet full also of the old Gospel. Be sure you say the old Gospel; we want no new one." Barrows's instincts concurred, and he pored over Sankey hymnals to learn what the evangelist had found effective. He studied Sankey's demeanor, too. The British press praised his courtesy, dignity, pleasant manner, and "perfect naturalness." "Shake hands with him," one reporter wrote, "exchange a few words, and you find yourself trying to accept the music for the sake of the man. How much we owe to him. Before his time the idea of preaching through song scarcely existed." Such efforts to articulate an effect beyond description awakened Barrows's vision for evangelistic music ministry alongside Graham. Barrows soon discovered that some British congregations still used Sankey's trailblazing hymnal *Sacred Songs and Solos* (1877). Compiled in response to popular demand, the book offered 1,200 selections, defined a core body of gospel hymns, and sold briskly from the start. Known popularly as "Sankeys" or as the "Sankey-Moody hymn book," *Sacred Songs and Solos* had its American counterpart, a compilation known as *Gospel Hymns 1-6*.

Barrows's reading also brought an appreciation for another successful song leader, Charles Alexander. A native of East Tennessee and a Moody Bible Institute-trained singer, Alexander served as song leader for two noted evangelists, J. Wilbur Chapman and R. A. Torrey. Known as a man who "had the happy knack of making a congregation sing," Alexander resonated with a description that appeared in the *Advance*: he had "a smile that wouldn't come off," and his genial manner accompanied an earnestness about gospel proclamation that made him, like Sankey, an effective minister in his own right to audiences around the world. His solos, simple in music and verse, touched hearts. People said of Alexander, as they had of Sankey, that he was the main attraction to the meetings. Contemporaries considered him "without a peer in the realm of modern evangelism." John MacNeil, the "Scottish Spurgeon," called him "the incarnation of music . . . and not only of music but of the Spirit of God, using Gospel songs as an instrument of blessing. He set our heartstrings strumming."

Known for "smiles, stories, and spiritual bonhomie," Alexander was the first music evangelist to feature piano rather than organ accompaniment. The culture craved entertainment, and whether or not he acknowledged it, Alexander delivered. Alexander gave people a good time before the earnest gravitas of R. A. Torrey descended upon the podium. He made revival music the reason to attend a crusade, pitting congregation against choir or men against women to see which group sang loudest, requesting impromptu solos from audience members, or using antiphony to sustain interest. He took Charles Gabriel's "Glory Song" as his theme: "Oh, that will be glory for me. . . . When by his grace I shall look on his face, that will be glory, be glory for me." When Alexander died in 1920, the *Sunday School Times* remarked that, thanks largely to Alexander, the "Glory Song" (written in 1900) had already appeared in print seventeen million times.

A series of hymnals called *Alexander's Gospel Songs* resourced his meetings and sold by the millions. Other favorites they popularized included "I Stand All Amazed," with the line "Oh, it is wonderful that He should care for me enough to die for me," and "O What a Change," with "Oh, what a change . . . when I shall see His face." While some royalties from his booming hymnal sales went to Moody Bible Institute, more lined the entrepreneurial Alexander's pockets.

Evangelical journalist G. T. B. Davis, who diligently reported on Protestant "forward movements" around the world and brought comparative awareness of revivals to his writing, made these observations in *Zion's Herald*: "I never saw any one conduct congregational singing like Alexander. He has that peculiar quality that we call magnetism because we have no better word. But he does make the people do exactly as he wants them, and he can interpret music. There was in it the thought and feeling of everyone in that choir, but the feeling in every singer was Alexander's own feeling transmuted. We have no singer now in America that is Alexander's equal in conducting congregational singing."

During evangelistic meetings with R. A. Torrey in Bendigo, Australia, in 1902, Alexander met Robert Harkness, a young Australian piano prodigy whom he recruited to travel with the Torrey-Alexander evangelistic team. Harkness hailed from a family of Methodist preachers and in time preached some himself, but he could usually be found at the keyboard. He considered the simple chords of gospel songs musically uninteresting and began improvising, ultimately creating a new model for aspiring gospel pianists. "His long, slender, practiced fingers swept the keys like a magician's," wrote a writer for the *Herald of Gospel Liberty*, "improvising melodious variations which tinkled and thrilled with birdlike harmonies delighting the ear." He proved a perfect partner for Alexander's upbeat music style and thrilled crowds with his keyboard prowess. When World War I brought worldwide revival tours to an abrupt end, Harkness settled in the United States and devoted the remaining sixty years of his life to music evangelism, traveling in concert, founding a music publishing house, and composing 2,500 hymns. His *Harkness Piano Method of Evangelistic Hymn Playing* (1941) set the standard for generations of gospel pianists. Barrows found much to admire in this musical team and in Harkness's accompaniment style. He concluded that Alexander's easy way with an audience, his friendly demeanor, his insistence on excellent accompaniment, and his reputation as a man with a big heart explained why people willingly traveled great distances to see him "melt and mold" a congregation. Barrows would have large shoes to fill.

As Barrows read about these earlier musical evangelistic giants, he could compare their methods and style to someone that both he and Graham knew personally: Homer Rodeheaver. By the 1940s, "Rody" was indisputably the living legend of gospel musicians. Rodeheaver had spent over twenty years warming crowds for Billy Sunday's energetic sermons and had developed his entrepreneurial instincts into endeavors that kept his own name before an adoring public. Music publisher, conductor, soloist, composer, trombone player, recording artist, and speaker, Rodeheaver traded his humble southern Ohio beginnings for a busy life in the public eye. He lived near the Sundays in Winona Lake, Indiana, and enjoyed a national reputation that brought him many invitations like the one he accepted in 1937 to lead an audience of eighty thousand crowded into Chicago's Soldier Field for the Chicagoland Music Festival in a "neighborly singing" of popular American songs like "Old Black Joe," "Moonlight and Roses," and "When I Grow Too Old to Dream." Christian Endeavor youth sang his songs at enormous conventions, while fundamentalist congregations everywhere purchased Rodeheaver Publishing Company hymnals. Rodeheaver was so well known at the grassroots level that a hardware store in Kansas promoted a "ladies parlor" with records featuring Rody favorites like "The Great Judgment Morning" and "Brighten the Corner Where You Are." Rodeheaver ran summer schools of music with a focus on improving congregational singing and made a point of encouraging the young evangelists active with YFC. Barrows naturally studied the man and his methods.

Rodeheaver's personality as well as frequent YFC meetings at Winona Lake eased the way. Rody was personable, outgoing, hospitable, and encouraging. Each summer crowds of church musicians flocked to Winona Lake to learn from the master. His lakeside home featured a slide from its roof to Winona Lake, and a visit to Rodeheaver was likely to combine recreation, hearty food, and instructive conversation. Barrows admired how Rodeheaver used what the *Chicago Tribune* had called his "tempestuous" trombone to keep tempo in large auditoriums, a helpful practice before adequate amplification became available. Like Sankey and Alexander,

Rodeheaver wanted everyone in his audiences to sing. Reporters estimated that during his career he led live audiences tallying at least seventy million people in song, calling him "the prince of conductors." Rodeheaver did not aim to promote music appreciation, nor did he seek out guest artists who sang to impress. Rather, he insisted on wholehearted congregational singing sustained by his own interaction with the audience and accompanists. "His voice, with its appeal of sincerity in explaining a song grips your heart before he has sung a note," gushed a reporter for the *Herald of Gospel Liberty* in 1916. "The man's adaptability is his greatest asset." That adaptability won Barrows's admiration.

Rodeheaver's warmth and enthusiasm were obvious assets but did not account fully for his success. The *New York Times* called him "one of the most expert masters of crowd psychology in the country," but there was more. Despite his apparent spontaneity, Rodeheaver chose songs strategically, always had a song ready, and was particularly diligent in his selection of invitation hymns. Although he relied on many different invitation songs, he believed evangelists should use just one per service no matter how many times it had to be repeated as people moved forward. Rodeheaver suggested that changing hymns midstream interrupted the flow of response.

Rodeheaver's organization of mass choirs also piqued Barrows's interest. From appointing a music committee to keeping track of choir members to selecting suitable music—Rodeheaver had practical advice that ran the gamut. He recommended "better-grade and more difficult gospel songs" for the choir, since many presumably had some musical training and experience. He regarded every singer as essentially a "personal worker" engaged in the grand purpose of the rally or campaign—eliciting decisions for Christ. He urged prayer with the choir, recalling choir members' gratitude for devotional times. For any particular campaign he recommended a catchy theme song that could easily be whistled on the streets or hummed in the office. His long years of success made Rodeheaver a sought-after counselor, and Barrows was eager to listen.

In 1910, Rodeheaver, along with Sunday's pianist, B. D. Ackley, created Rodeheaver Music as an efficient way to control the music the two wrote. They signed exclusive contracts with two of the era's most prolific hymn writers, George Bennard ("The Old Rugged Cross") and Charles Gabriel (tune for "Brighten the Corner"). In 1937, Rodeheaver acquired the Hall, Mack Company of Philadelphia, along with the services of its manager, C. Austin Miles ("I Come to the Garden Alone"), combining under his oversight the talents of the most popular contemporary names in gospel hymnody. His firm sold millions of books and made Rodeheaver a multimillionaire, yet, even so, his personal sales never seriously rivaled Sankey's. Yet via his publishing endeavors, Rodeheaver held the copyrights to more than ten thousand hymns and expanded his gospel music influence even as it expanded his fortune. His preference was to purchase a hymn outright so that he could use it as he wished.

As a hymn publisher, Rodeheaver had a stake in promoting what was new, but he also believed in the timeless worth of classic hymns. Rody pleaded with music leaders to "keep alive" the "splendid old hymns" even as they made use of "the newest, best, most practical" gospel songs. Beginning in 1922, Rodeheaver's vast influence expanded further as the public flocked to his new Rainbow Records label. Everywhere he went, he drew from standard gospel hymns but kept evangelistic music current by introducing the wealth of new gospel songs that regularly came his way. Most were fun to sing and musically undemanding; many were unabashedly sentimental and reflected the influence of popular secular music. Easy parts for everyone with repeats in the refrains and just enough syncopation to keep them interesting made Rodeheaver's choices popular with audiences and appropriate to Sunday's populist preaching style. Sunday's theme song and Rodeheaver's most-recorded solo was Ina Ogden's jaunty "Brighten the Corner Where You Are." Its commonsense advice to make the best of life's circumstances won it a secular as well as a religious audience.

Rodeheaver's methods, philosophy, and wide-ranging endeavors gave Barrows much to consider. He appreciated Rodeheaver's demeanor, communication, honesty, and transparency, but he did not fully appropriate the older man's musical style or embrace the sentimental ballads that endeared Rodeheaver to thousands. Nor would he spin off businesses from his evangelistic work. Both Barrows and Shea treasured the personal access Rodeheaver gave them to some of the century's most influential gospel songwriters as well as the generous encouragement he offered.

During their winter in Britain, Graham and Barrows said they spent most of their time praying, studying, and preaching. They networked with religious leaders and congregations within the established Anglican

Church and the "Nonconformist" churches, gained a clear understanding of the challenges Christianity faced in postwar Europe, made lifelong friends, and were spiritually quickened, especially by their contact with Stephen Olford. Their trip ended with a three-day conference for youth leaders in Birmingham.

In April, the men headed home, where, despite intentions to rest, they plunged immediately back into a grueling schedule. Graham had announced his intention to refuse engagements for several weeks, but invitations poured in. People seemed eager to hear firsthand about evangelism in postwar Europe, and during his first few weeks at home, Graham spoke nearly every night. The next month found Graham and Barrows leading a YFC rally in Portland, Oregon. Less than a week later, the two appeared in Chicago.

In November 1947, Graham and Barrows opened a two-week evangelistic campaign in Charlotte. The invitation to Charlotte had reached them in Europe, and, though both were still on the YFC payroll, the Charlotte meeting was not sponsored by the organization and was much more than a YFC event. Rather, it was Graham's first big endeavor on his own, and for the first time it showcased Graham's budding plan for longer city-wide events that would allow time for people to hear, consider, and heed the evangelist's message. Graham contacted George Beverly Shea back in Chicago and invited him to be the soloist; when he agreed, a platform team came together that would remain together for almost sixty years. Live broadcast commitments still limited Shea's availability, and he arrived for the third meeting rather than the first. But the delay only served to fuel mounting excitement for the arrival of a nationally known radio and recording personality.

Graham's resolve to add Shea as a third member of his evangelistic team had crystallized during his European visit. Early in 1947, Graham had addressed a letter to Shea laying out his heart for an evangelistic ministry and begging the singer to join him. Graham assured him that—if he could see war-ravaged Europe—he would drop his radio work and come immediately. Shea's reply does not survive, but certainly on Graham's return, the two partnered more often—actually, the three, since Barrows was there, too—in YFC rallies that took them on adventurous, cross-country jaunts in automobiles and airplanes. Later in 1947, Graham wrote Shea again, this time a three-page, single-spaced letter:

George Beverly Shea (BGEA)

George Beverly Shea (standing at microphone) (BGEA)

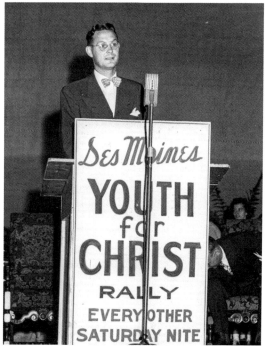

Torrey Johnson at Youth for Christ rally, ca. 1946 (BLASC)

Nurses' cross at Soldier Field, Chicago, during Youth for Christ rally, 1945 (BLASC)

Cliff Barrows (BGEA)

Cliff and Billie Barrows, mid-1940s (BGEA)

Billie and Cliff Barrows singing at piano while traveling with Billy Graham for Youth for Christ (BGEA)

Cliff and Billie Barrows with Billy Graham while traveling for Youth for Christ (BGEA)

Cliff Barrows at podium (BGEA)

Billy Graham and Cliff Barrows, late 1940s (BGEA)

George Beverly Shea, Billy Graham, and Cliff Barrows (BGEA)

Cliff Barrows, Stuart Hamblen, and Billy Graham (BGEA)

D. L. Moody and Ira Sankey (Library of Congress)

Homer Rodeheaver, ca. 1908 (Winona History Center, Grace College, Winona Lake, IN)

Homer Rodeheaver with chorus for Billy Sunday service, December 1916 (Library of Congress)

Billy Graham and Homer Rodeheaver, Winona Lake, IN, late 1940s (BGEA)

1973 crusade in Seoul, South Korea (BGEA)

Closing meeting of 1973 Seoul crusade (BGEA)

1949 Los Angeles crusade (BGEA)

Stuart Hamblen, ca. 1970 (Michael Ochs Archives / Getty Images)

Billy Graham at Melbourne, Australia, airport, February 12, 1959 (AP Photo)

Cliff Barrows leading the music at 1959 Southern Cross crusade (BGEA)

Walter Maier (BLASC)

Cliff Barrows and Billy Graham recording *The Hour of Decision* (BGEA)

Not only am I asking you to go with me because of your popularity around America and crowd-drawing appeal, which is tremendous, but also because of your spirit. When you sing, you preach the Gospel! You sing a sermon! There is a holy hush that comes over the crowd that is not true of any other singer in America that I know. . . . Your kindness, sweetness, humility and deep spiritual life commends itself immediately when you stand on the platform. When you get through singing, I am never worried about the results in the meeting. I feel that I can get up and—to use an expression Dr. Bob Jones often uses—"Preach the stars down." I believe that you and I and Cliff Barrows and a top pianist could go from city to city in gigantic city-wide campaigns that would be the greatest things this country has seen in twenty-five years.

Graham proposed to share any offerings equally with Shea and Barrows, but he promised as well that, if Shea preferred, he would guarantee Shea a salary of $10,000 ($112,000+ in 2021 dollars) and leave him free between campaigns for radio and studio work. However, he urged Shea to relinquish these endeavors and to share freewill offerings rather than retaining commitments that would divide his energies. Graham's confidence in his calling and his enthusiasm for the task he was about to undertake breathed through every line of the long letter. He urged the Sheas to take their time and prayerfully consider the proposal; however, he also thought he knew how they would respond: "I believe that God wants you in this thing, and I believe the Lord is going to show you." It did not take the Sheas long to recognize that Bev, Cliff Barrows, and Billy Graham, despite their very different gifts and abilities, shared a calling to one task. The men's calling had implications for their families, and the mutual regard and warm friendship the families enjoyed eased some of the stress occasioned by anticipated long separations and public demands. As things evolved and the future unfolded, though, Shea, while onboard for crusade duty, mapped out his own plan. For a few years he retained his radio and studio work while carving out time for Graham's growing number of crusades. In the mid-1950s, he resigned his radio responsibilities, but his studio work and concert schedule continued around the Graham crusades, enhanced by the wider visibility his association with Graham provided. Whatever his project, his billing would now include both "America's favorite gospel singer" and "Billy Graham's soloist."

By the time Shea was approached to come aboard, Cliff and Billie Barrows had already joined forces with Graham for the long haul. After the winter in Europe, they made a deliberate choice to set aside personal ambitions for collaborative work focused initially on congregational, choral, and solo music. From the outset, they intended a lifelong commitment. At twenty-four, Cliff Barrows became the personable host of Billy Graham's meetings with responsibility for all that preceded and followed the sermon. He—and, later, Shea—would affirm their lifelong commitments to one thing: promoting Billy Graham's ministry. Already in Barrows's short life, he had studied the history of hymns, pored over the biographies of their authors, met as many living hymn writers as possible, and learned all he could from his predecessors. What he gleaned from Sankey, Alexander, and Rodeheaver in particular contributed clear principles that came to guide his thoughts on music evangelism: (1) use songs with a purpose, chosen and sung to convict, encourage, comfort, exhort, and save; (2) aim for excellence (as Barrows put it, "if it doesn't sound good to the ear, it will not reach the heart"); (3) use music to unite and encourage people, enabling them to articulate common affirmations and resolve (and be sure that you pay attention to the theology of every line); and (4) use music to worship and glorify God. He liked to quote Charles Alexander: "Sing to save," and "Sing as if you were preaching, not singing."

However, just as the team-of-three took shape, Graham found himself roped into an unlikely and unsought role as a college president. Longtime fundamentalist firebrand William Bell Riley was in rapidly failing health and had set his eye on the dynamic young Graham to be his successor at the helm of his Northwestern College in St. Paul, Minnesota. Personally pressured by Riley and his circle, Graham reluctantly agreed that such an important opportunity must be God's calling, whether he wanted it or not. Riley passed away in December 1947, and the very next month the twenty-eight-year-old evangelist became the youngest and, likely, least enthusiastic college president in the United States. Ill-suited by temperament and ambition, Billy Graham's heart and calling were in evangelism, not in hosting social events, chairing meetings, or fund-raising. Not surprisingly, from the beginning he was a largely absentee president, relentlessly pursuing evangelistic opportunities while exasperating the administration and faculty of the struggling college. Graham would officially retain the helm of

Northwestern College for four years until the faculty petitioned him to step aside in favor of someone who could devote himself to the president's job. No one was more relieved than Graham himself when he stepped down in early 1952.

In the meantime, the reluctant college president maintained a relentless schedule of travel and preaching that included a brief return to London in the spring of 1948 for a YFC conference. That May Graham joined prominent evangelical leaders at the Chicago convention of a new cooperative agency, the National Association of Evangelicals. In June, King's College in upstate New York awarded him his first honorary doctorate. Late in the summer, he returned to Europe for meetings in Switzerland, a brief appearance as an observer at the organizational meeting of the World Council of Churches in Amsterdam, and YFC rallies in several cities. In August 1948, Barrows and Shea joined him for a crusade in Augusta, Georgia, followed by another near Cliff Barrows's old stomping grounds in Modesto, California.

When Barrows and Shea joined Graham, each brought experience that would shape the music of Graham's crusades. Shea's years as a Christian broadcaster and solo artist gave him a good feel for audience response to music. His name was already prominently associated with many songs he used frequently. Thousands of requests by letter and hundreds of concerts in congregations of every denomination in Chicagoland helped him grasp the effectiveness of particular texts and tunes. Occasional unhappy experiences with radio station accompanists shaped clear expectations of what he wanted going forward, and his vast repertoire of gospel songs and hymns made it easy for him to find something appropriate for any occasion. But there was more.

Adam Shea died in 1946, and Beverly Shea would live out his long life and his musical ministry in the glow of his father's memory—Adam Shea, the evangelist, who had impressed on his eight children that God's purpose for them "comprehended a living together with him in fellowship, in communion, in a passion for his service." Bev Shea embraced his father's example and found in his family's heritage of Wesleyan distinctives rich resources for knowing, experiencing, and serving God. He believed these molded his "sense" of an individual service and, as he put it, what God wanted him to do in it. Barrows and Graham grasped what Shea meant.

Their encounter with Stephen Olford heightened their own eagerness for what they called fellowship with God and empowerment by the Holy Spirit. The three men would be the only ones with the freedom to alter the components or flow of a crusade service. Barrows prepared orders of service that frequently left Shea's solo titles blank because Shea's "sense of the service" might well alter what he sang. Even the accompanists did not always know. Shea used a hand signal to indicate the key he wanted; they gave him a chord; and then they accompanied whatever he sang, allowing him full control of tempo and delivery.

Barrows brought to the trio boundless energy, a teachable spirit, and a quick mind. He, too, acknowledged a lifelong debt to his parents, who encouraged him to memorize hymns, develop his musical interests, and prioritize evangelism. They set the immediate example, but along the way he learned as well from Moody, Sankey, and other giants of the past. Barrows liked to quote Ecclesiastes 4:12, saying that a "threefold cord is not easily broken," and that he, Graham, and Shea were inextricably linked. Each had a distinct calling; Graham would be first among equals; and each man's endeavors would be devoted to the same goal. Each man's individual gifts made their common vision thrive. Each sought the other's flourishing and cherished the personal and ministry ties that bound them, and so a recognizable crusade sound emerged from their mutual respect, trust, and unity of purpose. From 1949 until 2005, they were the platform trio at the heart of every crusade. When their lives in the public eye ended, each still maintained that he had lived out his calling and had no regrets. In the fall of 1949, the "threefold cord" of Graham, Barrows, and Shea began a new chapter in their ministry partnership.

3

MINISTRY

Come, sinner, come to Jesus;
His word was meant for you;
His grace receive, his promise believe,
And sing his praise anew.

—"A Story Sweet and Wondrous," Eliza Hewitt, 1890

I n the fall of 1949, Graham, Barrows, and Shea accepted an invitation
to Los Angeles for a series of tent meetings that traditionally marks the
launch of their sustained common endeavors. The event began on September 27 under the banner "Christ for Greater Los Angeles." Despite a
surfeit of advertising, the meetings got off to a disappointing start, with
unusually cold weather curbing local enthusiasm for tent meetings. After
a few weeks, however, momentum built, until the press labeled what happened in the modest tent in an empty lot at the corner of Washington and
Hill Streets "six sin-smashing weeks."

From this "official" beginning of the Graham team's crusades down
to their final crusade in New York City in June 2005, Barrows and Shea
would hold forth over a coherent philosophy and approach to their music ministry. But obviously the logistical and contextual how and why of
crusade music would change over the years as settings moved beyond the

initial three-thousand-seat canvas venue of 1949. Success and fame would eventually lead to events like the 1973 outdoor rally in Seoul, South Korea, where one million souls sat under their voices, and decades of meetings in the world's largest stadiums, with simulcasts beamed to millions around the globe. A brief look at two crusades ten years apart—Los Angeles in 1949 and Australia in 1959—demonstrates not only how Graham's reputation grew and the nature of the crusades changed, but how the setting and use of the team's music evolved. In that first decade, simple beginnings yielded to meticulous procedures and organization building necessitated by Graham's rapid rise from up-and-coming itinerant revivalist to famed global evangelist and iconic cultural figure.

Coming into the Los Angeles meetings in late September 1949, Barrows had—compared to his prior YFC engagements—a relatively large pool of musical talent from which to draw. The physical setup of the tent stage made it evident that music would hold a prominent place. A pair of grand pianos sat near an electric organ in space crowded with placards bearing the slogans typical of most evangelistic campaigns since the early 1900s: "Jesus Saves," "My Life for Christ," "Jesus Keeps," "We Would See Jesus," "Behold, Now Is the Accepted Time; Now Is the Day of Salvation."

The pianists were Billie Barrows and Gladys Csehy, each well trained and experienced. A local prodigy named Lorin Whitney agreed to play the electric organ. Whitney had enormous natural talent. He began learning music after his family attended every evening of Aimee Semple McPherson's 1923 citywide Fresno revival. The boy professed conversion at the Full Gospel Tabernacle, a revival spin-off of a Pentecostal congregation affiliated with the Assemblies of God. After piano lessons with a local teacher, Whitney asked permission to practice on the organ of a local church. Within a few years, he enrolled at Southern California Bible College (Assemblies of God) in Pasadena and then found his calling as accompanist on the *Haven of Rest* radio broadcast. Opening his own studio in nearby Glendale, Whitney was well connected and well liked across the Los Angeles area and had long since crossed over into the region's fundamentalist networks; he proved a fine choice as the first crusade organist.

Barrows relied heavily on other local talent as well. He invited popular singers associated with the two best-known national radio broadcasts beamed from Los Angeles—the Haven of Rest Quartet and the Old-

Fashioned Revival Hour Quartet, along with the latter's virtuoso pianist, Rudy Atwood. One memorable night, the *Old-Fashioned Revival Hour*'s inimitable radio evangelist Charles E. Fuller led the crowd in his signature chorus, "Heavenly Sunshine," along with "Meet Me There," another of his nationwide radio favorites, supported by his Old-Fashioned Revival Hour Quartet. Fuller's booming, untrained voice roused the audience and sent a clear message that the music in a Graham crusade was for everyone, not just the practiced voices that dominated the platform ensembles.

Crusade crowds thrilled to many of the lively gospel songs radio audiences loved, and quartet members sometimes doubled as soloists. Cliff and Billie Barrows sang duets—"That's Why I Love Him So," "Jesus Has Promised My Shepherd to Be," "It's Real"; Shea and Barrows delighted the audience with "This Little Light of Mine," a number they repeated often over the years, sometimes with Graham booming out "No!" to the question, "Hide it [my light] under a bushel?" Shea rendered one gospel classic after another, sometimes as many as four or five numbers in a single service: "Softly and Tenderly," "Holy Spirit, Faithful Guide," "I Will Sing the Wondrous Story," "All That Thrills My Soul Is Jesus," "Jesus Is the Sweetest Name I Know," "Is There No Comfort for Sorrow?" "I Saw One Hanging on a Tree," "Jesus Paid It All." Many Protestants knew these familiar songs, and Shea's renderings showed that they remained useful for evangelism despite the growing murmurs from critics who considered gospel hymns "entry level" and regretted people's unwillingness to leave them behind in favor of the "meat" of traditional hymnody. Shea interspersed a few songs of his own compositions: "Sweet Rose of Sharon," "Blue Galilee," and, of course, "I'd Rather Have Jesus." Guest instrumentalists included the husband of pianist Gladys Csehy, concert violinist Wilmos Csehy, whose unique interpretations of hymns thrilled the crowd, and Los Angeles area YFC favorites, the Collins Twins.

The singing began spontaneously each evening as the audience gathered with "Shall We Gather at the River?," "In the Sweet By and By," and other well-known numbers. As people exited the tent, the singing continued on the streets. Barrows dismissed each service with the crusade's catchy theme chorus, "Send a Great Revival in My Soul," and newspapers reported that departing crowds sang it over and over on buses and trolleys as they made their way home:

Chapter 3

Send a great revival in my soul;
Send a great revival in my soul.
Let the Holy Spirit come and take control
And send a great revival in my soul.

Los Angeles had a track record as a difficult city for evangelism, and Graham's slow start seemed par for the course. Several thousand people attended during the early weeks, but the tent was never filled. Three weeks into the crusade, though, everything changed. The Hearst newspapers sent reporters and then increased coverage, the weather warmed, and instead of closing early, the crusade was extended several times, finally concluding on November 20 after an eight-week run. Thousands converged on the meetings, necessitating an extension to the tent that doubled its capacity, and still people crowded outside the raised tent flaps to participate. As momentum grew, a few prominent converts joined the hundreds who moved forward every night. There was local mobster Jim Vaus as well as Olympic distance runner Louis Zamperini (later immortalized in the book and film *Unbroken*). Another was Stuart Hamblen, a man whose change of heart would leave its mark on crusade music.

One of America's legion of "singing cowboys," Stuart Hamblen began his ascent to national fame in 1926 on Ft. Worth's WBAP and its Dallas sister station, WFAA. Reared in a Texas Methodist preacher's household, he had relocated to Hollywood by 1929 and was gaining fame as radio's "Cowboy Joe" as well as being "Dave" in the Beverly Hillbillies, Los Angeles radio's wildly popular western singing group. From 1931 on, he emceed some of the premier radio programs on the West Coast, including *King Cowboy and His Woolly West Revue*, *Stuart Hamblen's Covered Wagon Jubilee*, *Stuart Hamblen and His Lucky Stars*, and, later, *The Cowboy Church of the Air*. A regular supporting actor in movie westerns alongside John Wayne, Gene Autry, and Roy Rogers, Hamblen also hosted the popular radio show *Family Album* and was the first western artist to sign with Decca Records.

Despite his phenomenal singing, broadcasting, and acting successes, Hamblen's hard living and hard drinking led to frequent arrests for disturbing the peace. Troubled by her husband's destructive behavior, Suzy Hamblen began attending a recently formed evangelistic outreach called the Hollywood Christian Group, a Christian witness to people in the entertainment industry. Suzy found supportive friendships in the group that sustained her as she prayed for her husband's conversion; the group had close ties to First Presbyterian Church of Hollywood and its dynamo director of Christian education, Henrietta Mears.

At least since the 1920s, the congregation at First Presbyterian had flourished under the able preaching of Dr. Stewart P. MacLennon and his successor, Dr. Louis Evans. Evangelistic programs multiplied under the innovative leadership of Mears, an educator, speaker, and author whose commonsense approach to Christian education revolutionized the field. Under her supervision, Sunday school and youth ministries blossomed at First Presbyterian. Mears invested herself especially in the church's hundreds-strong college group, and her biographers claim that she influenced some four hundred of "her boys" to enter the ministry. Mears founded Gospel Light, a publishing house that produced her graded Sunday school curriculum, and she established Forest Home, a conference center situated in a high valley under the shadow of Mount San Gorgonio in the San Bernardino Mountains. After World War II, Mears turned her attention to reaching Hollywood's actors, producers, writers, and film crews.

Several people in the film industry already attended "Hollywood Pres," among them Colleen Townsend (later Evans), a recent convert who had signed with Twentieth Century Fox. At a Forest Home conference in 1949, Townsend vowed to share her faith in her workplace. Several other film industry employees soon made similar commitments. Tim Spencer, cowboy singer/songwriter and a founding member of the acclaimed singing group the Sons of the Pioneers, was another celebrity who turned from alcoholism and professed faith at the church. In a short time, they created the Hollywood Christian Group.

Billy Graham also came under the influence of Mears at Forest Home in the late summer of 1949. Challenged by his friend and onetime colleague Charles Templeton to come to terms with modern biblical scholarship, Graham was wrestling with the fundamental question of taking the Bible as God's Word. He settled his doubts during long talks with Mears and even longer times alone in prayer on the mountainside: he left Forest Home determined to preach the Bible as God's Word, whether he understood all of it or not. Just a few days later, he opened his now legendary Christ for Greater Los Angeles crusade.

Mears, meanwhile, invited a small but growing group of entertainers, including new converts Roy Rogers and Dale Evans, and actress Jane Russell, to meet in her living room in nearby Westwood (where Mears counted Rita Hayworth and Douglas Fairbanks Sr. among her neighbors) to decide how to approach their colleagues in the industry. They agreed to sponsor alternate Monday night gatherings open-by-invitation-only to employees of the entertainment industry. Every other Monday, the core group would meet for prayer; alternate Mondays would have an evangelistic focus. Meetings moved from home to home and attracted a growing number of participants and many casual visitors. As his first crusade got under way, Graham addressed the Hollywood Christian Group, making connections that would turn out to benefit the crusades in the years ahead. Among his contacts were Suzy and Stuart Hamblen, who, at his wife's urging, occasionally accompanied her to the Monday evening gatherings.

Graham wrangled his way onto Hamblen's radio show as part of precrusade publicity and extracted a promise from Hamblen to attend a crusade service. Although Hamblen recognized the need to put his life in order, he had been resisting the overtures of the Hollywood Christian Group and kept his promise to Graham only with great reluctance. After enduring a troubled conscience for days, Hamblen finally called Graham's hotel room one night well after midnight. (The team's presence kept the hotel operators busy: the hotel estimated that on average two phone calls per minute came in for Graham, Barrows, or Shea, around the clock.) Hamblen somehow got through to Graham, who invited Hamblen to his hotel room, where they talked and prayed until Hamblen surrendered his life to Christ. When he attended the crusade that evening, Hamblen came as a platform guest rather than as a conflicted seeker. The next day he announced on air that he was "hitting the sawdust trail." He sold his racehorses, gave up alcohol, and became something of a curiosity among his friends. A few days later, Hamblen's father arrived in Los Angeles to give public thanks in Graham's pulpit for his son's conversion. Graham later recalled Hamblen's conversion as a breaking point in the crusade: audiences and general interest increased once Stuart Hamblen gave his testimony.

Hamblen now joined his wife willingly at the Hollywood Christian Group, where both found a growing network that sustained their faith over the next several years. Hamblen became a temperance advocate and ran as the Prohibition Party's presidential candidate in 1952. His refusal to allow alcohol ads on his popular shows cost him major sponsors. He eventually launched his own Christian broadcast, *The Cowboy Church of the Air*, that ran for fifteen years.

The news of Hamblen's about-face provoked comment and questions among his Hollywood friends. One evening, the Hamblens visited their next door neighbor John Wayne, and the conversation came around to recent changes in Hamblen's lifestyle. Reacting to astonishment at the change that had come over him, Hamblen replied to the effect, "It is no secret what God can do." "That is a beautiful thought," Wayne said, and challenged Hamblen to write a song on the subject. As the clocks chimed midnight, the Hamblens crossed the lawn to their home. Hamblen went directly to his study, picked up a pen, and completed the song in about fifteen minutes. In the years that followed, the song reached a varied cross-over audience, spending time in the top ten in both the pop and sacred charts, and was later recorded by such artists as Elvis Presley. Translated into more than ninety languages, "It Is No Secret" would be used many times in Graham crusades around the globe, with Hamblen often traveling to meetings to sing his song as a solo and a testimony.

The song intimates Hamblen's own travails, his struggles, before extolling the courage and strength God can give the troubled soul; he'll never allow you to walk alone, Hamblen sings, nor will he allow any power to conquer you.

> It is no secret
> What God can do;
> What he's done for others
> He'll do for you.

Crusade advertising had flooded Los Angeles's airwaves and newspapers, but perhaps none of it approached the effectiveness for Graham's meetings of the popular radio and film star's appearances. Hamblen's move from mourner's bench to crusade pulpit had major implications for the music in future crusades. He became the first of a long line of legendary entertainers who brought their established reputations and their publics under the sound of Graham's voice. When Hamblen succumbed to brain cancer in March 1989, Billy Graham preached his funeral.

Nearly a decade after that first Los Angeles crusade, Graham, Barrows, and Shea—accompanied by associate evangelists and a sizable staff that had already been on the ground for a year—opened four months of meetings in Australia and New Zealand. The longest and most ambitious effort yet in Graham's growing list of global endeavors, the Southern Cross Crusade of spring 1959 revealed much about the professionalization of the ministry in its first ten years. Crusade music had become streamlined during this period. Although it consumed less time on the program, it retained its place within the core of each service.

A smoothly run crusade relied heavily on Barrows and his team. Barrows knew what Graham preferred and made choices with Graham in mind. By 1959, Barrows had proved himself the chief catalyst, the "can do" partner in making crusades happen. Often best remembered for his platform roles at crusades, Barrows was equally engaged behind the scenes. More than anyone except the evangelist himself, he had the vision for the logistics of a whole crusade from start to finish. He was there to do everything humanly possible to enable Graham to focus on preaching, and he maintained this demanding mind-set for sixty years. The first to arrive and the last to leave each service, he served as the chief advance man, coming and going before a crusade, and as a cleanup man at the end. From the earliest planning stages, the Southern Cross Crusade relied on his firm but genial guidance.

By 1959, a handbook detailed the organizational apparatus for each crusade, delineating the expectations for local committees and the contributions of the Billy Graham Evangelistic Association (BGEA—formed 1950). A music committee in each major crusade city recruited choir members and arranged rehearsals. Local crusade organizers made certain that Australian and New Zealand bookstores carried books about Billy Graham, records by George Beverly Shea, and write-ups of prior crusades. Barrows's office at the BGEA in Minneapolis obtained necessary copyright permissions, prepared a hymnal for crusade use, worked on shipping and customs requirements, consulted local crews on platform arrangement and choir seating, procured suitable instruments, and made sure an adequate sound system was in place. Transmission of crusade services over telephone lines to Australia's remote settlements required meticulous preplanning, as did contingency plans for crusade audio in overflow venues. Activities in host cities crowded daytime hours before evening services, and scheduling the team in churches and meeting venues presented another set of logistical challenges. Barrows solicited advice from local Australian and New Zealand music committees about hymn favorites and preferred tunes as well as suggestions for suitable accompanists and singers for meetings undertaken by associate evangelists.

A few months before the team arrived, Australian radio began featuring Shea, making his voice familiar long before he and his fellow Canadian, pianist Tedd Smith (who joined the team in 1950), arrived for a few precrusade events. By 1959, precrusade concerts had become a custom that attracted thousands and built anticipation for what followed. In the United States, they typically occurred months before the meetings, but in locations abroad, they were often part of the immediate lead-up to the services. Barrows arrived ahead of the meetings to rehearse choirs and review the physical arrangements for each service. Several months earlier, local organizers had secured airtime on forty Australian radio stations for *The Hour of Decision* (first broadcast in 1950), another way of beaming the message and music and building crusade anticipation. Movies documenting crusades elsewhere ran in churches and theaters in major cities. Posters, a house-to-house visitation program, and press coverage made it difficult to escape awareness of the Southern Cross Crusade.

Graham flew into Sydney's Mascot Airport on February 11, 1959, where a throng of reporters and hundreds of eager admirers jammed the overseas terminal. He was merely passing through en route to Melbourne, but a palpable excitement rippled through the crowd. Later that night some two thousand people sang Fanny Crosby hymns outside the evangelist's room at the Wentworth Hotel. Sydney's welcome turned out to be a mere prelude to Melbourne's demonstrative embrace the next day.

When Graham arrived in Melbourne, hundreds of people clad in their "Sunday best" swarmed Essendon Airport and greeted the evangelist by singing lyrics from crusade favorites, Crosby's "To God be the glory, great things He hath done" and "Blessed assurance, Jesus is mine." They followed Graham from the tarmac to the lounge, where scores of reporters and photographers waited. After a brief meeting with the crusade executive committee, Graham patiently spent two hours at an airport press conference before being whisked off to his hotel. Groups of people cheered his motorcade along the way. The press rewarded Graham with upbeat news coverage, and editorials chimed in with enthusiastic support. The Victoria

Palace Hotel provided the tall evangelist with a custom-made seven-foot bed, and five Melbourne golf clubs issued complimentary memberships. Outside the hotel, several thousand people created a massive traffic jam, singing "To God Be the Glory" as police cleared a path for Graham to enter the hotel. "Preacher Gets a Film-Star Welcome," one headline read the next day. By all indications, a celebrity had arrived, and something noteworthy was about to happen. Music had already played a vital role in channeling anticipation.

By 1959, impromptu hymn singing had become an unorchestrated part of welcoming Graham and his team. Two Fanny Crosby hymns, "Blessed Assurance" and "To God Be the Glory," were so woven into the crusade fabric and so well known by laypeople, that they became the preferred vehicle for expressing the excitement that mounted as a crusade approached. Both songs had emerged as crowd favorites during the London crusade in 1954 when Barrows used "Blessed Assurance" as the crusade theme song. Barrows's discovery and use in England of "To God Be the Glory," a Crosby song then little known in the United States, initiated the hymn's rise to popularity in every later crusade.

The Southern Cross Crusade opened on an unseasonably chilly Sunday afternoon, February 15, 1959. Hours before the first service, police estimated that a line six to eight people deep stretched for half a mile. When the stadium doors opened, seats filled quickly, and thousands stood outside to listen over a public address system. As the service got under way, a heavy downpour diminished the outdoor crowd, but at least five thousand stayed. Graham later came out to address them in person, and ninety-seven people from the overflow crowd responded to his invitation. The actual service followed what had become the usual crusade template—a welcome and invocation by the local chairman, who turned the service over to Barrows; a solo by Shea; Scripture reading; prayer; introduction of Graham and distinguished guests; choir number; offertory by pianist Tedd Smith; congregational hymn; a second Shea solo; sermon; invitation with choral background of "Just as I Am"; benediction.

Barrows's compilation, *Crusade Songs*, a paperback hymnal containing fifty-nine choir selections ranging from gospel choruses to familiar hymns, as well as a larger pamphlet with ninety-eight selections for general crusade use, sold briskly. A generous number of easy-to-sing gospel songs like

"A Wonderful Savior Is Jesus My Lord" and "Since Jesus Came into My Heart" found a place among old favorites like "Jesus, Lover of My Soul," "A Mighty Fortress Is Our God," and the old revival meeting favorite, "All Hail the Power of Jesus' Name."

Each service concluded with the mass choir singing "Just as I Am," and in three weeks in Melbourne more than 26,000 people came forward. The final service overflowed the Melbourne Cricket Ground with an estimated attendance approaching 140,000. Graham read greetings from President Dwight D. Eisenhower and was flanked by high-ranking local officials. When the final prayer ended, the massive audience rose to bid Graham and his team farewell with the song "God Be with You 'Til We Meet Again." All told, some 730,000 attended the Melbourne meetings in person while untold thousands more listened in forty-five local and distant communities via landline relay or radio.

Next, the team moved on to Tasmania and New Zealand. Again, singing crowds welcomed them at airports. A Maori youth choir from the United Maori Mission provided local color at Auckland, where three thousand awaited Graham despite his midnight arrival. New Zealand had its own separately published crusade hymn collection. "Blessed Assurance" took pride of place as the hymn on the first page, with "To God Be the Glory" at the end. This strategic placement made it easy for Barrows to announce his favorite crusade selections. When Graham, Barrows, and Shea departed Christchurch for the next event in Sydney, more than 1,100 people lined the way from the terminal to the plane, singing "Blessed Assurance" and "How Great Thou Art." The songs functioned as a summary of crusades, blending anticipation and outcomes that differed in detail but corresponded in essence everywhere.

In 1959, the Sydney area was home to a fifth of Australia's ten million people. Graham began with a precrusade gathering of a thousand clergy and four hundred laypeople, during which he deflected critics by admitting deficiencies in mass evangelism and acknowledging his dependence on local churches to reap the crusade harvest. Then the marathon began. In the four weeks that followed, twenty-six services attracted nearly a million people. The local Catholic hierarchy and press warned their faithful to stay away if they valued a clear conscience, but other Catholics loudly defended their presence in Graham crowds. Behind the scenes, luncheons, preaching engagements, university visits, clergy conferences, and press events occupied every spare minute. From the 50,000 who attended the opening service to the 150,000 who jammed the Showground and the adjacent Sydney Cricket Ground to hear Graham's sermon, "Two Ways and Two Masters" (Matt. 7:21-27), at the final service, Sydney's citizens turned out in droves. Landlines drew in audiences in over three hundred locations deep in Australia's "bush country" and a hundred miles up the coast to Newcastle. To the astonishment of "sober churchmen," the *Christian Century* observed, citizens of New South Wales were "talking religion on buses and ferries."

Despite intermittent rainfall and a raging flu epidemic that affected some 30 percent of the population, the final service attracted Australia's largest audience to date for any single event, filling both the Showground (circa 80,000) and the adjoining Sydney Cricket Ground (circa 70,000). Hours before the 3 p.m. start time, both stadiums had standing room only. The logistics that enabled the final service were staggering and testified to Barrows's ingenuity. Graham, Shea, and Barrows participated in person in both stadiums while public address systems united the vast audience. Shea and two choirs, 1,500 voices at the Showground and 2,000 linked by miles of cable and one hundred amplifiers from the cricket ground, sang "How Great Thou Art." Graham preached a sermon entitled "The Broad Way and the Narrow Way" and gave the invitation to people in two stadiums at once. Then he remembered those listening via landline relays and instructed them to move to the front of their particular auditoriums. More than 5,600 people came forward in the rain in the neighboring stadiums alone. Then, as earlier, the altar call took time. The choir repeated "Just as I Am" as thousands moved forward; massive crowds meant that the singing lasted nearly thirty minutes.

Graham's associate evangelists next departed Sydney for shorter engagements in Perth and Brisbane. After a few days of rest, Graham, Barrows, Shea, and accompanist Tedd Smith followed to participate in the concluding services in each city. When it was all over, Graham told the *Sun Herald*: "Today marks the close of the most wonderful four months of my life." The team went their separate ways. Graham flew out of Sydney for London. At least five thousand people stood in the rain to send off the evangelist with the singing of "How Great Thou Art." Upon landing in London, Graham found yet another singing throng greeting him with "Blessed Assurance."

These songs had become emblematic of crusades, and they also suggested the important role that music played in every meeting and in crusade preparation and follow-up events. Why did crowds around the world welcome the team with the same two or three songs? Why did thousands gather at any time of day or night, rain or shine, to sing them without direction or accompaniment?

Of course, music had historically played a pivotal role in past revivals. The grand hymns of Charles Wesley and John Wesley's masterful hymnal with its plainspoken instructions for singing emerged from the throes of an eighteenth-century revival. In the 1870s, sources suggest that Ira Sankey's gospel songs were hummed, whistled, and sung wherever people gathered. Barrows often remarked that Christianity was a singing faith. A plaque featuring a quotation from Martin Luther hung on the wall in the Barrowses' home: "Next to the Word of God, music deserves the highest praise. The gift of language combined with the gift of song was given to man that he should proclaim the Word of God through music."

No particular songs stood out, however, the way that "Blessed Assurance" and "To God Be the Glory" did among Graham's public. Certainly, Barrows's frequent use of these two Fanny Crosby hymns played a part in the sense of their appropriateness at crusade-related events, as did Crosby's firmly rooted place in modern Protestant song. Crosby's name evoked an indefinable "something" that recalled her persistence amid physical challenges and personal heartache as well as her well-known participation in evangelistic efforts. Simply put, people knew that Crosby resourced revivals, and this feeble woman had for decades offered Protestants a vocabulary for their Christian lives. In Australia, Barrows identified "Blessed Assurance" as Graham's favorite hymn. (Graham's reputed favorites ranged widely over nearly sixty years of crusading.) The song was widely sung and widely translated, giving it a global reach long before Graham crusades began. Its words captured the heartbeat of Graham's platform team and neatly combined their music goals: worship, testimony, exhortation. Its emphasis on praise supported Barrows's particular focus on the joys of the Christian life.

"To God Be the Glory" fit similar criteria, and its lyrics added the dimension of global outreach: "Let the earth hear His voice" alongside "Let the people rejoice." People sang both songs easily because they were familiar, but they "said" crusade because of their frequent crusade use, and that use came about because they aptly captured the essential crusade message and set it to singable tunes. The platform team favored music that focused on God rather than on self, and Barrows used both songs as congregational hymns. Everyone sang them in crusades; at the same time, the songs themselves *sang* the crusade's one message. After its use in New York's Madison Square Garden in 1957, "How Great Thou Art" filled a similar function.

The ten years between the Christ for Greater Los Angeles campaign and the Southern Cross Crusade brought enormous changes to crusade media, planning, and music organization. In 1949, most of the people involved in the music were longtime friends or local acquaintances who willingly pitched in to make the campaign work. By 1959, most crusades were long, complex events governed by processes and networks that had evolved with the ministry. The Southern Cross Crusade required many musicians—guest artists and accompanists—intricate planning, massive recruiting, and attention to new media possibilities. Amid the changes, at least two critical features remained constant: Barrows and Shea were always there, and the basic music repertoire remained the same. Whatever else happened, Barrows and Shea would strike the note that *said* Graham crusade. Whoever else came long, they carried the brand name as they had since the opening meeting in Los Angeles. And the hymns and gospel songs the team preferred in 1949 continued to serve them well a decade later. They remained known and loved expressions, and anchoring the crusades in familiar songs and vocabulary was another way of tying into the Christian cultural memories that still echoed in many places where Graham preached.

From their modest beginning, Graham crusades had quickly become massive happenings attracting record crowds to the world's largest venues. The BGEA displayed legendary organizational savvy and singleness of purpose. As the three men fulfilled their one ministry, they influenced the emergence of modern global evangelicalism in spoken and sung words that told and retold the one story that defined them.

4

SOURCES AND INFLUENCES

Gimme that old time religion,
Gimme that old time religion,
Gimme that old time religion,
It's good enough for me.

—Author unknown, "Old-Time Religion," 1873

W hat became the unmistakable musical sound of Graham's crusades in its first years emerged within the rich historical context of a varied, yet always evolving, evangelical music. The Graham musical team drew upon classic hymns that were mainstays of Sunday worship, revived once-loved gospel songs that had gone out of fashion, and frequently promoted new compositions that emerged from the flourishing ranks of evangelical songwriters and publishers. In the process they created a distinctive musical profile that reflected the treasured shared history of their publics, while also being open to new approaches that were gaining favor within the evangelical tradition.

The Impact of Religious Radio

One of the most important new musical influences on traditional Protestants in the years just prior to, and surrounding, the Graham crusades' emergence came from exciting developments on the nation's airwaves. By the 1940s, radio listeners across the country had a growing choice of religious broadcasts, and the most popular among them featured innovative musical artists who had figured out a musical style suited to the medium of radio. They knew that timing, diction, tempo, and accompaniment mattered if listeners were to keep the dial tuned to their program. Judicious use of music had become a sure way to attract an audience, lock in a signature sound, and build a lucrative following.

As someone with years of experience in broadcasting, George Beverly Shea had a keen interest in all aspects of the emerging medium. While the expectations of his employers at WMBI and then on *Club Time* structured his day-to-day responsibilities, he, like Graham and Barrows, followed in the wake of big-time regional and national Protestant broadcasters who became fundamentalist household names in the 1930s and 1940s. The Graham platform team benefited immensely from the popularity of these Christian radio personalities who commanded large audiences and whose broadcasts featured a message and musical idioms the Graham team admired. Among these were four in particular who had decades of staying power and ever-expanding audiences on the radio: Walter A. Maier, Paul Myers, Charles E. Fuller, and Theodore Epp. Each program not only reflected the dynamism and skills of its featured evangelist but also had a distinctive musical sound and a set of favorite songs made familiar across the country via radio and recordings. They helped shape the context for Graham's crusade music and often assisted directly in his early crusades. As part of its context, and as occasional partners, they constituted an important part of the early biography of crusade music.

The Lutheran Hour, The Haven of Rest, the *Old-Fashioned Revival Hour*, and the *Back to the Bible* broadcasts attracted their audiences from the same people that yearned to hear traditional hymns, lively gospel music, and musical innovations by accompanists and singers. Despite their popularity, however, all four programs—and conservative and fundamentalist Protestant broadcasts in general—faced hostility from the liberal-leaning

Protestant Federal Council of Churches, which led a campaign against paid religious broadcasting. The Council viewed itself as the legitimate voice of the nation's respectable Protestant establishment and relished its role as the clearinghouse for national Protestant broadcasts. For many years they received free "public service" network time on NBC for *The National Vespers Hour*, featuring Harry Emerson Fosdick, pastor of Manhattan's Riverside Church, and for the *National Radio Pulpit*, with fellow New York pastor Ralph W. Sockman. Shut out from the limited availability of free national network opportunities, conservative Protestants fought a long uphill battle to assert the right to buy time on national networks in the same way they purchased airtime on local stations. Their most vocal and determined ally was Walter A. Maier, the popular speaker on *The Lutheran Hour*.

Maier had impeccable academic credentials, but two Harvard graduate degrees, remarkable facility in ancient languages, and competency in Old Testament scholarship did not deter him from pursuing first and foremost his call to the Lutheran ministry. He grasped the potential of radio and in 1930 launched *The Lutheran Hour*, the first denominationally sponsored (by the Lutheran Laymen's League of the Lutheran Church–Missouri Synod) national religious broadcast. His academic credentials provided access to influential forums, publications, and cultural influencers, and he used every opportunity to make a case for paid religious broadcasting.

Maier preached a forthright evangelistic message filtered through a distinctively Lutheran lens that kept law and gospel in focus. Maier arrived at the studio in a suit, but before he approached the microphone he removed jacket, tie, shirt, and belt, flexed his arm muscles, and then preached in T-shirt and slacks. A fine speaker, he was keenly aware of the limits and advantages of the medium, and Graham and Shea both observed his techniques. Broadcasting placed time constraints. Every minute had value, and his message had urgency.

Like his cohorts with roots in American revivalist denominations, though, he recognized the importance of music. *Lutheran Hour* music had a much more "churchly" sound than did his fundamentalist contemporaries and provided yet another option within the musical influences that shaped the Graham team. Each program was usually bookended by the rich strains of "A Mighty Fortress Is Our God" and "Beautiful Savior," both translations of classic German hymns, and the broadcast also made time for numbers by a Concordia Seminary choir. Maier made *The Lutheran Hour* a phenomenal success. When he died in 1950, the program commanded a larger potential radio audience than any other broadcast, sacred or secular. Among the tributes that poured in when Maier died was one from Billy Graham, a young man then on the cusp of his career, who recognized in Maier a kindred spirit for evangelism and a mentor in radio evangelism.

During the late 1920s, Paul Myers was a Los Angeles radio manager and broadcaster who enjoyed a loyal following. But in the early 1930s, a growing dependence on alcohol abruptly derailed his career. In a skid row hotel near the San Diego docks, Myers happened on a Bible placed by the Gideons (an evangelical businessmen's group organized in 1899 to distribute Bibles). He began reading and soon professed conversion. Myers returned to his family and his secular radio work with a new purpose. In 1934 Myers launched a religious radio broadcast he called *The Haven of Rest*, taking his theme from a gospel song composed in 1890 by the Northern Irish-born immigrant Henry Lake Gilmour. A Methodist hymnal editor and camp meeting choral director, Gilmour described an endangered soul adrift on life's sea who found an anchor in Christ:

> My soul in sad exile was out on life's sea
> So burdened by sin and distress
> 'til I heard a sweet voice saying "Make me your choice,"
> And I entered the haven of rest.
>
> REFRAIN
> I've anchored my soul in the haven of rest
> I'll sail the wide seas no more;
> The tempest may sweep o'er the wild stormy deep
> In Jesus I'm safe evermore.

Myers resonated with the poem, and he adopted its nautical imagery—even to the point of donning a captain's uniform—for his radio evangelism. His public knew him as "First Mate Bob on the Good Ship Grace"; listeners were "shipmates," and one by one he recruited a quartet that he dubbed "the good ship's crew." Myers first aired *The Haven of Rest* on March 16, 1934, with Lorin Whitney at the organ. In 1941 he constructed a nautical-themed broadcast studio with portholes for windows, upper and lower decks, a gangway ramp, and deck handrails. (In 2007, the city of Los Angeles designated the building a historic monument.)

The Haven of Rest's music won the program instant popularity. The Haven of Rest Quartet, four young men who serendipitously discovered that they sounded good together, offered at least four gospel songs on each daily broadcast (live in studio from 1934 to 1950), and organist Whitney played a solo in the middle of the program (he and two quartet members were students at the Assemblies of God's local Southern California Bible College). The program's distinctive sound found an immense audience that grew along with the frequent release of records, especially the new 33-1/3 rpm LPs that debuted in the late '40s. Sometimes a cappella and sometimes with organ accompaniment, the Haven of Rest Quartet became known for its crisp sound and its sensitive renderings of standard hymns and newer gospel songs. "I Once Was Lost in Sin," "The Old Rugged Cross," "It Is Well with My Soul," "There's Room at the Cross for You," "Yesterday, Today, Forever," "A Shelter in the Time of Storm," "He Hideth My Soul," "He Lifted Me," "Victory in Jesus"—these standards and many more underpinned Myers's preaching in musical selections that reiterated his spoken words.

Shea admired the Haven quartet's music and was a regular listener. They popularized a musical sound similar to that which Shea promoted first on his own radio shows and later at Graham crusades. Gilmour's "The Haven of Rest" became one of Shea's most requested solos. When the Graham team organized their crusade in Los Angeles in 1949, Lorin Whitney was a natural choice as the Graham team's first organist.

On October 3, 1937, another gospel broadcast destined to reach across the nation and then around the world aired for the first time from a Hollywood studio. A weekly hourlong Sunday broadcast, the *Old-Fashioned Revival Hour* featured Charles and Grace Fuller, pianist Rudy Atwood, organist George Broadbent, a choir, and a quartet. The Fullers presented a serious message in a folksy family style. Veteran local broadcasters, they mastered the use of the medium before they took their efforts nationwide.

Fuller devoted fully half of the program to singing, and his mail attested that listeners found the music irresistible. The greater Los Angeles area provided him with an enormous pool of highly trained musicians with professional experience and training, and he made the most of their talents. When Fuller went live and moved his broadcast to the Long Beach Municipal

Auditorium, the draw of the music only increased. Thousands filled the auditorium, millions tuned in each week, and millions more purchased records featuring the choir, the quartet, and the unmistakable accompaniment of Rudy Atwood (who became a solo recording artist in his own right). Some people admitted that they came primarily to watch Atwood as his hands raced through octaves and arpeggios. Widely admired for his ornamental playing, Atwood became a model for innumerable aspiring gospel pianists.

Alongside Priscilla Owens's stirring 1898 hymn "We Have Heard the Joyful Sound," Fuller used his own "little chorus," "Heavenly Sunshine," as his opening theme:

> Heavenly sunshine, heavenly sunshine,
> Flooding my soul with glory divine!
> Heavenly sunshine, heavenly sunshine,
> Hallelujah, Jesus is mine!

During the broadcasts, Fuller frequently interacted with his live audience and his musicians. His rendition of Fanny Crosby's "Meet Me There," sung along with the Old-Fashioned Revival Hour Quartet, became an audience favorite. Fuller was not a singer, but he enjoyed participating wholeheartedly in ways that endeared him to his crowds. The Old-Fashioned Revival Hour Quartet supported Fuller's preaching much as Shea's solos would later support Graham's. The broadcast gave visibility to old and new gospel songs and hymns, all performed in a style at once lively yet decorous with accompaniment that made them memorable.

Fuller made enormous contributions to the spirit and substance of the emerging new evangelical movement. He spoke at YFC events, supported Graham's earliest crusades, and in 1947 established Fuller Theological Seminary, a school that captured the hopefulness of newly energized evangelicals eager to win the world to Christ. He was in the thick of the network out of which Graham emerged. Behind the scenes, interactions among Fuller's and Graham's musicians influenced the performance style of gospel singing.

On May 1, 1939, another influential program, *Back to the Bible*, first aired from Omaha, Nebraska. Its speaker, Theodore Epp, was a Mennonite pastor who had learned the broadcasting ropes from T. Myron Webb, the Oklahoma-based speaker on the weekly *Bible Fellowship Hour*. Webb was an evangelist who had eventually become the radio voice of the Free

Methodist Church in the 1940s and popularized newer gospel hymnody through his weekly broadcast from Seattle Pacific College. During a visit to his family back in Nebraska, Epp discovered that there was a dearth of gospel radio programming in the state. He resigned his Seattle-area pastorate, told Webb he was moving on, and settled in Lincoln to explore his options. He convinced a station manager that listeners needed to hear "something for the heart" and accepted an offer for a fifteen-minute daily slot. The signal was weak, but the cost was just $4.50 per program.

Epp steadily added stations, and his broadcast went international via shortwave in 1943 on missionary station HCJB in Quito, Ecuador. Epp incorporated his efforts as Good News Broadcasting Association, and by the mid-1960s, *Back to the Bible* could be heard over stations that covered much of the world. Music was perhaps the key ingredient for Epp's broadcasts. Each program opened with a rousing rendition of "I Love to Tell the Story," a well-loved nineteenth-century gospel song by Katherine Hankey. As Epp developed a regular format, soloists, a Back to the Bible Choir, and a male chorus often sang, but the most popular group was the Back to the Bible Quartet. Utilizing unpretentious arrangements and simple harmonies, the quartet's style put the spotlight squarely on their songs' lyrical content. Although the group did not neglect classic hymns, the bulk of their songs were tried-and-true gospel songs like "Springs of Living Water," "He Wore a Crown of Thorns," and "Only Jesus."

In 1950, Graham, Barrows, and Shea launched their own radio broadcast, a half-hour weekly program known as *The Hour of Decision*. After years of close observation of conservative Protestant broadcasters, they opted for a format that echoed a Graham crusade. Hosted by Barrows, it typically featured a solo by Shea, a crusade choir number, and a message by Graham. Widely syndicated, for sixty-six years the program distilled the essence of a Graham crusade and made it available weekly to a global audience.

Musical Connections

If the national broadcasts featuring talented musicians were one source of Graham crusade music and one standard of performance style, Shea's own radio experience, his YFC appearances, and his sacred concert opportunities were another. Many numbers that became classics at Graham crusades featured prominently in Shea's endeavors well before *Songs in the Night* brought Shea and Graham together. Shea's connections at Moody Bible Institute and his interactions with Homer Rodeheaver's musical circle expanded his repertoire, and he helped popularize newer or less widely known songs in concerts, recordings, and broadcasts. One prime example of how this collaborative process worked was the story of the song "Then Jesus Came," by Toronto pastor and evangelist Oswald J. Smith.

The overlapping networks that anchored Shea in Chicago reached back into his native Ontario, where Smith was taking his place as one of Canada's leading evangelicals. Smith was many things—preacher, poet, missionary, evangelist, author—and he made the People's Church in Toronto a busy center of support for North American evangelical endeavors. Some one hundred of his poems became hymns, but their contemporary influence depended on their exposure on the widest possible stage. Graham's musicians found suitable songs among Smith's writings. The story of one that Shea popularized around the world reveals how friendship connections became productive in musical gospel work.

The key figure in making that happen was Homer Rodeheaver, whose vast hymn-publishing empire and record company could give any gospel hymn enormous exposure. One of his friends was Oswald J. Smith. One evening in 1939, Rodeheaver sat in the cavernous Billy Sunday Tabernacle at Winona Lake listening to the feisty fundamentalist debater Harry Rimmer speak about the "darkness" and "gloom" that entered the home of Mary and Martha upon the death of their brother Lazarus (John 11). After dwelling on the pain of sadness, Rimmer suddenly shouted: "Then Jesus came. That changed everything." Rodeheaver immediately recognized in "then Jesus came" the theme for a gospel song. A few days later, he traveled by train to Philadelphia, where his Rodeheaver Publishing Company had an office. He used the hours to work out the details of the song he imagined. Fortuitously, his business partner, pianist and composer B. D. Ackley, was at the piano in his office conversing with Smith (in town for a speaking engagement) when Rodeheaver burst in to share his idea.

Smith caught Rodeheaver's enthusiasm and delivered lyrics the next day. Rodeheaver quickly composed a tune, published the song, and began using it immediately in his own evangelistic services as an invitation hymn. Rodeheaver himself then recorded it, and when in 1959 radio personality

Paul Harvey decided to commemorate the sounds of early religious radio, he chose this solo as one of the selections for his LP *Yesterday's Voices*. When Shea began singing Smith's song on air, in solo engagements, and for Graham crusades, he guaranteed at least two more generations of familiarity. Of Smith's 1,200 poems, none achieved the acclaim that evangelistic use gave this one. Late in his long life, Smith addressed a warm letter of thanks to Barrows and Shea for the wide exposure they gave his work, especially "Then Jesus Came." Here is the refrain to that popular song:

> When Jesus comes the tempter's power is broken
> When Jesus comes, all tears are wiped away
> He takes the gloom and fills my heart with glory
> For all is changed when Jesus comes to stay.

Like Shea's personal testimony, "I'd Rather Have Jesus," "Then Jesus Came" became one of Shea's signature radio songs. During the crusade heyday, he sang it multiple times at every crusade and built a solid audience for Smith's lyrics. If popularizing the lyrics of contemporary hymn writers was one way that Shea built his repertoire, another way was reaching back to the tried-and-true successes of the past and keeping them alive for upcoming generations. Well before he joined Graham, Shea adapted Scottish author Elizabeth Clephane's posthumous words set to Ira Sankey's tune, "The Ninety and Nine."

Nothing more readily evoked the memory of Moody-Sankey meetings than did "The Ninety and Nine," a song Sankey singlehandedly made a classic. Shea sang it on the air and at YFC events, and Barrows used the song to great effect in Graham crusades, often as a solo by Shea or arranged for Shea and the crusade choir. The song was first used in Moody's meetings in Edinburgh, Scotland, in 1874 and became an immediate favorite. Included in Sankey's definitive gospel hymnals in the United States and Britain, it lived on in evangelical and fundamentalist hymnals. With his commitment to continuity with the gospel songs and the revivalists from earlier eras, and his eagerness for music that carried a message, Barrows found "The Ninety and Nine" an ideal crusade hymn. To early crusade audiences its gospel message was unparalleled: it wove together story and doctrine in a rendering of the biblical parable of the lost sheep. It was familiar, popular, and moving.

Chapter 4

A resident of Melrose, a picturesque village in the rolling hills of the Scottish Borders, Elizabeth Clephane wrote this and many other poems, and "The Ninety and Nine" (then known as "The Lost Sheep") received no particular notice when it first appeared. Sankey, while in Scotland, noticed it printed in the London paper the *Christian Age.* He cut it out and placed it in his pocket and went on to several days of meetings in the Free Church of Scotland Assembly Hall in Edinburgh.

Three days later, Moody preached on the parable of the lost sheep. The celebrated Scottish pastor and hymn writer Horatius Bonar (who wrote "I Heard the Voice of Jesus Say," among other songs) added some thoughts on the same subject, and Moody then asked Sankey for a solo suited to the topic. As Sankey later recalled it, nothing came immediately to his mind but the poem in his pocket—a poem ideally suited to the occasion but for which there was no tune. He placed the text on the organ, struck an A-flat chord, prayed, and began to sing. When he finished, Moody stood at his side, tears in his eyes, asking Sankey where he had obtained the song. Sankey wept, too, as Moody gave the benediction to the hushed crowd. And so a hymn was born from a poem that appeared only after its author's death, a poem that had no tune until its first performance as a hymn.

A few days later, Sankey received a note of thanks from Clephane's sister. Family members recalled that the poem had originally been written with a wayward brother in mind. Stories poured in about the song's effectiveness. Moody referred to the new song as "The Ninety and Nine" so often that Sankey changed the poem's title to match its popular designation.

> There were ninety and nine that safely lay
> In the shelter of the fold.
> But one was out on the hills away,
> Far off from the gates of gold.
> Away on the mountains wild and bare,
> Away from the tender Shepherd's care.
>
> "Lord, Thou hast here Thy ninety and nine;
> Are they not enough for Thee?"
> But the Shepherd made answer: "This of mine
> Has wandered away from me;

And although the road be rough and steep,
I go to the desert to find my sheep."

But none of the ransomed ever knew
How deep were the waters crossed,
Nor how dark was the night the Lord passed through
Ere he found his sheep that was lost.
Out in the desert he heard its cry,
Sick, and helpless, and ready to die.

"Lord, whence are those blood drops all the way
That mark out the mountain's track?"
"They were shed for one who had gone astray
Ere the Shepherd could bring him back."
"Lord, whence are Thy hands so rent and torn?"
"They are pierced tonight by many a thorn."

And all through the mountains, thunder riven,
And up from the rocky steep,
There arose a glad cry to the gate of Heaven,
"Rejoice! I have found my sheep!"
And the angels echoed around the throne,
"Rejoice, for the Lord brings back his own!"

This Sankey favorite had never really gone away, although by the mid-twentieth century it had lost much of its earlier popularity. But its renewal in Shea's hands gave it currency in a contemporary demographic that cut across denominations and generations and began to make it familiar again even before Graham's team came together. Despite (and maybe because of) his scant professional training, Shea found an enormous public devoted to his sensitive renditions of such gospel favorites.

Another song from Shea's pre-Graham career that his later global public embraced was "The Love of God," a song people identified with Shea several years before he linked up with Graham. Its subsequent use in Graham crusades turned this early twentieth-century poem into a mid-twentieth-century classic hymn. Fred Lehman, a German immigrant who spent much of his life in pastorates in the Midwest, wrote the lyrics in 1917. The song has a strange history—not just because it was first published in 1919 in a book called *Songs That Are Different, V. 2*—but also because the third stanza came from a ninety-couplet Aramaic poem, *Haddamut*, written in 1050 by Meir Ben Isaac Nehorai, a medieval Jewish cantor in Worms. They echo as well the Thirty-First Sura of the Qur'an (31:27).

Lehman first heard the medieval lines read at a camp meeting with an explanation that they had been found penciled on the walls of an insane asylum. Deeply moved, Lehman jotted down the text but did nothing with it for years. He passed through personally difficult times and in his later years found himself a manual laborer in Southern California. One day during a break, he laid a scrap of paper on an empty lemon crate and wrote the hymn that had been on his heart for years:

> The love of God is greater far
> Than tongue or pen can ever tell;
> It goes beyond the highest star,
> And reaches to the lowest hell;
> The guilty pair, bowed down with care,
> God gave His son to win;
> His erring child He reconciled,
> And pardoned from his sin.

> REFRAIN
> Oh, love of God, how rich and pure!
> How measureless and strong!
> It shall forevermore endure—
> The saints' and angels' song.

> . . . .

> Could we with ink the ocean fill,
> And were the sky of parchment made,
> Were every stalk on earth a quill,
> And every man a scribe by trade;
> To write the love of God above

Would drain the ocean dry;
Nor could the scroll contain the whole,
Though stretched from sky to sky.

Compare the words of the final stanza to this free translation of the *Haddamut*:

Even if all the heavens were parchment,
And all the reeds pens,
And all the oceans ink,
And all people were scribes,
It would be impossible to record
The Greatness of the Creator.

Even when time required abridging the song, Shea always included the final stanza, and he often sang "The Love of God" just before Graham preached.

Yet another old song that Shea appropriated to express his personal resolve to use music as gospel proclamation was Baptist pastor Francis Rowley's "I Will Sing the Wondrous Story." Written for local use at the First Baptist Church of North Adams, Massachusetts, in 1886, the song had little exposure until Ira Sankey recognized its potential and included it in his *Gospel Hymns*. Shea used it often, singing it very slowly to its original tune by hymn writer, evangelist—and portable organ manufacturer—Peter Bilhorn.

I will sing the wondrous story
Of the Christ who died for me;
How he left his home in glory
For the cross of Calvary.

REFRAIN
Yes, I'll sing the wondrous story
Of the Christ who died for me,
Sing it with the saints in glory,
Gathered by the crystal sea.

> I was lost but Jesus found me,
> Found the sheep that went astray,
> Threw his loving arms around me,
> Drew me back into his way.

Shea, then, had built a solid audience for his own renditions of what became his most popular Graham crusade solos long before crusades began. As a song leader who selected the music he directed, Barrows also became identified with particular numbers that he favored from the start. He used them in YFC rallies until he knew what tempo he preferred, which words to hold out, and which stanzas best suited his purposes. His favorites tended to be gospel standards, particularly those songs like Fanny Crosby's "Blessed Assurance."

Aunt Fanny

During her ninety-five years, Fanny Crosby (1820–1915) became a legend by composing thousands of hymns (many under a variety of pseudonyms) for Sunday schools, voluntary societies, Christian Endeavor (youth) conventions, and church and mission anniversaries. Known for her sunny disposition, she busied herself in New York City's rescue missions and made as little as possible of the blindness that had afflicted her from infancy. Ira Sankey sang dozens of Crosby's hymns in Moody's revivals and printed scores of them in his hymnals, but by the mid-twentieth century, many had passed from favor. Hymn publishing was in its heyday, and a constant sifting process made room for new items at the expense of older numbers. What often mattered most on the business side was the bottom line: independent hymn publishers assiduously developed the market for new numbers, and older numbers often languished.

By the 1930s, perhaps twenty of Crosby's thousands of hymns remained in common American use. However, many more that had declined in popularity in the United States remained widely known abroad. One such song that found a particularly prominent place in Barrows's repertoire was "Blessed Assurance." It was his favorite hymn, he said, until he learned "Great Is Thy Faithfulness," and he then acknowledged difficulty ranking the two. Barrows made the song so popular that it generally preceded crusades; throngs by the thousands greeted and farewelled the Graham team around the world with its familiar strains. At Graham's crusade at London's Harringay Arena in 1954, journalists remarked that every service began and concluded with its comforting words. It had been used with effect for a century, and now the Graham team gave it meaning for another generation. Its success in the crusades translated into recordings that further disseminated it—the Carter Family, Mahalia Jackson, Tennessee Ernie Ford, southern gospel great J. D. Sumner, CeCe Winans, Alan Jackson, and Cicely Tyson on Broadway were among the many who recorded versions of the song:

> Blessed assurance! Jesus is mine;
> Oh, what a foretaste of glory divine.
> Heir of salvation, purchase of God,
> Born of His spirit, washed in His blood.
>
> CHORUS (REPEATED)
> This is my story, this is my song,
> Praising my Savior all the day long.
>
> Perfect submission, perfect delight,
> Visions of rapture now burst on my sight;
> Angels descending bring from above
> Echoes of mercy, whispers of love.
>
> Blessed assurance! All is at rest;
> I in my Savior am happy and blest.
> Watching and waiting, looking above,
> Filled with His goodness, lost in His love.

The American publication history of this hymn shows its enduring popularity from the time Ira Sankey began using it in Moody's meetings in the 1870s. Written in 1873, it appeared in print first on the back cover of that summer's *Guide to Holiness*, the premier journal of the robust northern Holiness movement. Some believe it was first sung by the thousands in attendance at the 1873 camp meeting in Round Lake, New York.

The story behind the song revealed Crosby's versatility. Her friend and benefactor, Brooklyn socialite Phoebe Palmer Knapp, composed a tune, played it for Crosby, and then asked her what the tune said. Crosby immediately responded, "Blessed assurance! Jesus is mine." The three stanzas and chorus came to her just as easily as the first line, and in a few minutes, a new hymn was born. Crosby usually wrote text that composers later set to music. This was a rare instance when the tune came first. Like Barrows, Sankey had found "Blessed Assurance" an effective congregational song and made much use of it in Moody's meetings. He included it in the series of gospel hymnals he published, a series that became the definitive gospel song collection of his generation. Within months of its appearance, missionaries translated it for use overseas, so when the Graham team traveled beyond the English-speaking world, they found that this increasingly beloved American hymn was well known around the globe.

Barrows's encounters with British Nonconformists during the winter of 1946–1947 drew his attention to Sankey's lingering influence in such varied forms as the tradition of Scottish male-voice gospel choirs first formed in Glasgow as an activity for converts of the Moody-Sankey mission in the city in 1891. These concerts and recordings, known as Festivals of Male Voice Praise, kept the Moody revival favorites in public view over the years. Prominent among these songs were "Blessed Assurance," as well as other Crosby texts like "I Would Have the Savior with Me," "Behold, Behold the Wondrous Love," and "I Shall Know Him."

"All Hail"

As the older corpus of revival hymnody, including precedents established by Sankey, offered a ready source of crusade hymns, so did older gospel songs and hymns used by revivalists between Moody's death in 1899 and Graham's start in 1949. From Sankey forward, evangelists particularly found "All Hail the Power of Jesus' Name" a hearty and unifying number that aptly captured the goal of evangelism. In frequently highlighting "All Hail," Graham's musicians continued its use in a tradition stretching back to the eighteenth century and carried forward most recently by Homer Rodeheaver and Aimee Semple McPherson.

Well known throughout the English-speaking world and across denominations, the hymn had several popular musical settings, and its familiar lines accomplished Barrows's goal of uniting diverse crowds. Barrows used it for both choir and congregation, selecting the preferred tune of the local region. Many hymns of English origin carried British, Australian, and American tune preferences, and Barrows worked with local musicians to make suitable choices about tunes or, where necessary, translations. In addition to using it in crusade and concert settings, Barrows relied on "All Hail the Power" as a longtime theme song for *The Hour of Decision*, Billy Graham's half-hour radio broadcast. By 1955, just five years into its history, the program was broadcast on seven hundred stations with an estimated audience of 20 million, and its reach gave it a prominent role in the dissemination of crusade hymns.

The stirring lyrics of "All Hail the Power of Jesus' Name" aptly summarized Graham's Christ-centered message. Written at the height of the eighteenth-century revivals that shaped the evangelical movement, the song came from the pen of Edward Perronet, son of an Anglican vicar, whose French Protestant émigré ancestors had sought refuge in seventeenth-century England. The first stanza appeared initially as an anonymous poem entitled "On the Resurrection, the Lord Is King" in November 1779 in the *Gospel Magazine.* In April 1780, the same magazine published eight stanzas under the same title, again as an anonymous submission. Perronet did not acknowledge authorship until 1786. He subsequently also included the text in a small book of his poetry entitled *Occasional Verses Moral and Sacred. Published for the Instruction and Amusement of the Candidly Sacred and Religious.*

Evangelists—like most hymnal editors—found the full text far too long for ordinary use and usually incorporated a new, final stanza written by the English Baptist hymnist John Rippon in 1787. And so "All Hail the Power of Jesus' Name" evolved from poem to hymn with several common tunes and, on average, four or five stanzas.

> All hail the power of Jesus' Name!
> Let angels prostrate fall;
> Bring forth the royal diadem,
> And crown Him Lord of all!

Ye chosen seed of Israel's race,
A remnant weak and small,
Hail Him who saves you by His grace,
And crown Him Lord of all!

Let every kindred, every tribe,
On this terrestrial ball,
To Him all majesty ascribe,
And crown Him Lord of all!

O that, with yonder sacred throng,
We at His feet may fall,
Join in the everlasting song,
And crown Him Lord of all!

A Unique Sound and Mix

In Graham crusades, such grand old revival classics sounded quite different from what Sankey's and Alexander's crowds had heard. A grand piano and Hammond organ enlivened the singing, pianists employed the embellished style first popularized by Robert Harkness, and the latest amplification systems carried Barrows's voice and instrumental accompaniment to the farthest corners of stadiums. Music publishers like the Rodeheaver Hall-Mack Company, Zondervan, Lillenas, and Singspiration resourced the crusades by providing permissions and much of the choir music that lent uniformity to the content of crusade singing around the world.

Graham agreed with Barrows and Shea that a combination of older hymns and gospel songs best communicated the platform trio's message in a reverent and compelling way. Moody and Sankey laid the groundwork, and Graham's team took it from there, selecting from Sankey's classics a few they would make their own. Congregational singing provided the prime opportunity to enlist every audience member in a single activity, and Barrows made it part of every service—even when heavy rain occasionally shut down the piano and organ at outdoor stadiums.

The repeated use of particular numbers wherever the team traveled highlighted the heart of the religious content essential to an emerging global evangelical consensus. Thanks to missionaries, publications, and earlier evangelists, many American hymns enjoyed vast publics abroad; translations had long since interwoven them into local Christian cultures. People everywhere claimed them as their own. For each longer crusade, Barrows prepared a crusade hymnal—a collection of traditional hymns, gospel songs, and the newer choruses that gained favor in youth evangelism. In the '50s and '60s, Graham crusades lasted weeks rather than days, and crusade hymnals typically included some one hundred selections. Assembling the hymnals required a "sense" of crusade context, purpose, and message so that the song selection was adequate; permissions from different publishers; printing and shipping arrangements; and distribution (and collection) instructions for ushers at crusades. The books were also available for sale. Barrows oversaw all of this, and as crusades became ever more ambitious endeavors, music publishers cooperated with generous permissions and instrument vendors supplied their best pianos and organs for crusade use free of charge. In the shorter crusades of the 1980s and after, service music was included in the daily handout.

The titles that stood front and center throughout decades of crusades show the types of older songs for which both men reached. Of course, they used familiar numbers like "Amazing Grace" (which Shea often introduced with a few words about John Newton); Charles Wesley's majestic "Love Divine, All Loves Excelling"; and the 1650 Scottish Psalter's rendering of Psalm 23. They regarded such hymns as timeless. They set out to associate Sankey favorites with their own work, among them "Blessed Assurance," "To God Be the Glory," "All Hail the Power of Jesus' Name," and "The Ninety and Nine." In addition were the many familiar gospel hymns Shea sang as solos and then recorded. "I Come to the Garden Alone," "Count Your Blessings," "My Anchor Holds," "Ivory Palaces," "'Tis So Sweet to Trust in Jesus," "The Old Rugged Cross," "All That I Want Is in Jesus," and "Jesus, Keep Me Near the Cross" were just a few of his long list of beloved hymns.

Shea and Barrows relied heavily on their skilled accompanists, whose arrangements and harmonization enhanced the message without showcasing their own formidable musical skills at the expense of lyrics. Of this changing cast of characters, Tedd Smith and John Innes served for decades. (Smith replaced Billie Barrows, the team's first pianist, whose growing family claimed her attention, in 1950 and remained until 2004.) Throughout his decades on crusade platforms, Shea occasionally felt inadequate because of his lack of formal training. Guest artists featured highly skilled musicians whose talents Shea thought dwarfed his own. The people who mattered most—Graham and Barrows—begged to differ, but Shea consistently downplayed his musicianship. He commented in a note to Smith, "Since 1909 Winchester days [the year and place of his birth], I have not climbed very high, but it is because of real musicians such as you that I have even been on the trail." But Shea's contribution to crusade continuity with the hymns of the past was immeasurable. Even more than the choir and congregational songs, his repeated use of older standards kept those songs in print, on the radio, and in people's musical vocabularies.

Barrows and Shea believed that music encouraged worship and united hearts and minds. They chose music with a message, music intended to encourage people to come to a moment of decision about the Christian life. The hymns that fit their criteria were in one sense unremarkable and strikingly familiar—either "tried and true" numbers or newer songs of similar style—but early observers noticed two differences. First, Shea's performance style and his ability to make a song preach a sermon without calling attention to himself lent a sincerity and seriousness that contrasted with much familiar revival music. A writer for the *Hymn* observed: "When Shea steps to the pulpit and with deep reverence begins to sing 'I'd Rather Have Jesus,' you understand in a small measure the reason for the success of the team."

Second, an unscientific but suggestive survey of the content of the songs Sankey, Rodeheaver, and Barrows published for evangelistic use revealed continuity and change over time, confirmed shifts in the broader religious culture, and indicated Barrows's affinity for Sankey over Rodeheaver. Fully a third of the songs Sankey and Barrows selected exhorted and invited people to "come to Jesus," whereas Rodeheaver devoted just one in five songs to that category and included far more numbers that featured Christian warfare and victory. Sankey and Barrows allotted equal space to songs of doctrine and faith, far more than did Rodeheaver. The analyst discovered that only Rodeheaver included songs that touched on contemporary politics (prohibition was a lively issue in his heyday). Barrows used no "senti-mental songs"; Sankey included a few; but Rodeheaver's audiences could count on them. Death and judgment loomed large among Sankey's choices but commanded far less space in Barrows's collections. Barrows introduced three times as many "songs of joy and rejoicing" as Sankey, and more even than Rodeheaver (whose jaunty theme song "Brighten the Corner Where You Are" certainly struck a lively note). Barrows took songs like "What a Fellowship, What a Joy Divine," "There's within My Heart a Melody," and Charles Fuller's "Heavenly Sunshine" to elicit recognition of the joys of the Christian life. He managed remarkable variety in these small compila-tions by tailoring every selection to the crusade purpose. From "Trust and Obey"; to "It Is Well with My Soul," "What a Friend We Have in Jesus," and "I Stand Amazed in the Presence"; to songs of the second coming ("Is It the Crowning Day?"); to invitation classics ("Almost Persuaded" or "I Can Hear My Savior Calling"), these paperback collections admirably served as congregational hymnals and crusade mementos that kept the music alive in families and congregations long after the team moved on.

As Graham's worldwide audiences grew, so did Barrows's use of hymns that spoke in particular ways within certain cultures. At a mammoth meet-ing in Berlin's stadium soon after World War II, he realized that "A Mighty Fortress Is Our God" resonated in German Protestant souls. In India, "I Have Decided to Follow Jesus" was meaningful because it derived from a period of persecution of Indian Christians in the mid-nineteenth century. "He the Pearly Gates Will Open" was a popular number in Scandinavia: Shea and Barrows typically sang the chorus as a duet in Swedish. Crusade music offers many glimpses into how songs from one region or ethnic her-itage expanded their reach into global audiences. The occasional African or Spanish number, or Negro spirituals—sung either by Shea or by Afri-can American guest artists—expanded the musical repertoire. The issue of cultural appropriation never surfaced—and may well never have even occurred to anyone at the time—even in the wide press coverage. Few com-plained that Shea simply could not render an African American spiritual with authenticity: people appreciated what he did with spirituals (which he loved to sing). In France, Shea used spirituals instead of hymns: despite his father's bilingual upbringing, Shea refused to sing in French and offered instead a selection of spirituals already popular with the audience.

At the same time, Barrows was becoming increasingly attuned to the more contemporary sound of pop-influenced songs from the 1960s forward. This was seen in Barrows's interest in the popularity of the music of Bill and Gloria Gaither as well as new favorites produced in the 1980s and 1990s by baby boom recording artists like Michael W. Smith and Amy Grant. He had a remarkable ability to include popular new tastes, diversifying crusade music while preserving its signature sound. His own and Shea's continuity made that possible. Whatever else might happen, Shea's solos and Barrows's choirs, along with "Just as I Am," anchored the musical sound. Occasional appearances by the Gaithers were one thing: Shea's rendering of Gaither favorites like "He Touched Me" made the song fit his usual style.

Graham crusade music, then, had varied sources. It developed in a context where popular radio broadcasts shaped expectations about sound and style, and it relied on the overlap between the principals of the Graham team and the musicians of the busy evangelical music world around them. Crusade music drew on the revival tradition, on the broad experiences in radio and YFC that shaped Shea and Barrows, and on new material that reflected the continuously evolving musical tastes of a changing evangelical culture. Both men had a formidable knowledge of hymnals and hymn writers. They knew their musical and cultural contexts and cast an eye to the contemporary expectations of their audience. And so crusade music adapted multiple traditions to pursue its one goal.

Since crusades featured congregational and choir singing as well as solos—and since crusade music was also recorded and marketed—people rightly associated a long list of songs with crusades. But there would be two songs that stood apart and defined the Billy Graham crusade musical tradition and experience.

THEME

Why do I sing about Jesus?
Why is he precious to me?
He is my Lord and my Savior;
Dying he set me free.

—"Why Do I Sing about Jesus?" Albert Ketchum, 1923

The *Christian Century* noticed very early on that the Graham team was about "one thing." The editors attributed their phenomenal rise to that single-mindedness. Fanny Crosby, one of the men's heroes, provided a thumbnail essence of that "one thing" in her beloved 1875 hymn, "My Song Shall Be of Jesus":

My song shall be of Jesus, the precious Lamb of God,
Who gave Himself my ransom and bought me with His blood.

Every individual crusade song the Graham team selected was essentially a variation on one song that focused on redemption and invitation. This Christ-centered intention suffused the songs, sermons, prayers, and testimonies that filled each fast-paced service. It was especially prominent in two of the iconic hymns identified most closely in the public mind with a Billy Graham crusade: "Just as I Am" and "How Great Thou Art." In several publications that the BGEA distributed to donors and sold to the public, Barrows rehearsed the stories of these defining songs. They, too, functioned as crusade story.

"Just as I Am"

Graham, Barrows, and Shea had been personally moved by "Just as I Am" long before they became a ministry team, and they chose from the start to conclude each service with a hushed rendering of its solemn invitation and assurance of pardon for sin. This consistency set Graham crusades apart. Most evangelists relied on several invitation hymns, often suiting them to the sermon topic. Since Graham, Barrows, and Shea served together for nearly sixty years, their unvarying use of the same song at every service gave "Just as I Am" a secure, specific, and well-known role in the crusade ritual. Graham believed that at that moment of invitation, Barrows and he functioned as one: "When I would begin the invitation and Cliff would lead in singing 'Just as I Am,' he was just as much part of what the Holy Spirit was doing in people's hearts [as I was]."

First published anonymously in 1836 in the British magazine the *Christian Remembrancer*, "Just as I Am" was set to its common tune in 1849 by the talented American musician William Bradbury (who also wrote the tunes for "Jesus Loves Me," "He Leadeth Me," and "Savior, Like a Shepherd Lead Us," among others). By the time Graham, Barrows, and Shea adopted it as the Graham crusade invitation hymn, the song had a long history of use in evangelism in multiple languages. Used consistently throughout the length of his ministry, "Just as I Am," with its words sung and tune hummed as Graham urged people to make a decision, indelibly linked both its words and melody with the crusades. The Graham crusade's primary contribution to the hymn's story was consistency in use and in sound until the song "said" Graham crusade to millions. In early crusades, the congregation sang "Just as I Am" as people moved forward for prayer. Later the song became a choir number.

"Just as I Am" arose out of a particular personal experience that had nothing to do with evangelism or revival. Its widespread use in modern times invites a brief look at its English origins as well as an exploration of how an intensely personal poem became an internationally favored hymn. Charlotte Elliott, the author of "Just as I Am," was born into comfortable circumstances in London in 1789. The granddaughter of Henry Venn, founder of the (Anglican) Church Missionary Society, Elliott stood at the center of a prominent evangelical Anglican circle that included such notables as the celebrated Cambridge preacher Charles Simeon and the eloquent antislavery activists William Wilberforce and Zachary Macauley. The Clapham district of south London was the nerve center of this form of Anglicanism that joined personal piety and social action, and Elliott came of age in a home shaped by religious fervor attentive to both inward and outward religion. Hymnologist Louis Benson aptly described the "Clapham Sect" as a group that put the gospel first and the church second: attentiveness to ritual counted far less than inward and outward conformity to New Testament principles. Through her youth and early adulthood, Elliott neither participated fully nor rebelled outwardly; she admired the piety that surrounded her but had a keen sense of her own personal unworthiness.

One day in 1822, Cesar Malan, a Swiss visitor to the Elliott home, asked Charlotte if she knew Christ as her Savior. She resented the question and dismissed it with the comment that religion was a private affair. A few days later, she regretted her curtness and apologized with the admission that she did not know how to "take Christ" in that way. Malan said simply, "Come to him just as you are." Those four words—"just as you are"—stamped themselves in Elliott's mind. Years later the visitor's response became the genesis of the hymn.

Despite the surer faith Elliott now sensed, she struggled with growing physical limitations. In 1823 she moved to Brighton to reside in the household of her clergyman brother, Henry Venn Elliott, who was establishing a school for the daughters of clergy at St. Mary's Hall, Brighton. The family devoted themselves to projects to fund the venture, but Elliott's sense of physical helplessness, this time accompanied by deep doubts about her relationship with God, afflicted her again. After one restless night, Elliott spent a day in her room recalling the certainties of her faith and, among them, her long-past conversation with Cesar Malan. That morning she wrote the poem "Just as I Am." In the afternoon, her sister-in-law Julia Elliott (herself a hymn writer) came to her room, and Charlotte showed her the poem. Deeply impressed, Julia took the poem to a bazaar being held that evening to benefit St. Mary's Hall. Early printings of Elliott's poem suggest that she did, indeed, contribute to the fund-raiser she desperately longed to support: its heading read "Sold for the benefit of St. Mary's Hall, Brighton."

In 1835 a philanthropically minded English woman paid for the poem's preparation as a leaflet to circulate as a tract. No author was listed, and one day a copy found its way back into Elliott's hands with the recommendation, "I am sure this will please you." Shortly thereafter, "Just as I Am" appeared anonymously in an "unpretending magazine," the *Christian Remembrancer*, in 1836. In any publication where Elliott had influence with the editors, the poem was printed under the text, "Him that cometh unto me I will in no wise cast out" (John 6:37). In 1841, the words were printed as a six-stanza hymn in *The Invalid's Hymn Book*, a collection Elliott rearranged (and expanded with 115 of her own poems) at the request of an Irish friend.

The hymn took its final seven-stanza form with its publication in an edition of Elliott's *Hours of Sorrow Cheered and Comforted* (1849). The noted English hymnologist Erik Routley described "Just as I Am" as a "simple expansion of the single word, 'Come,' the most familiar and persuasive of all the gospel imperatives." An American hymnologist called it "a masterpiece of metrical gospel." Elliott treasured a letter from Edward Quillinan, husband of English poet laureate William Wordsworth's beloved daughter Dora, who described how "Just as I Am" comforted his wife during her prolonged final illness. Sent to Dora by the daughter of Robert Southey, another poet laureate and Lake District poet, Elliott's lines became, Dora often said, "her prayer—the very thing for me."

> Just as I am—without one plea
> But that Thy blood was shed for me,
> And that Thou bid'st me come to Thee—
> O Lamb of God, I come!
>
> Just as I am—and waiting not
> To rid my soul of one dark blot;
> To Thee whose blood can cleanse each spot—
> O Lamb of God, I come!

Just as I am—though tossed about
With many a conflict, many a doubt;
Fightings and fears within, without—
O Lamb of God, I come!

Just as I am—poor, wretched, blind;
Sight, riches, healing of the mind,
Yea, all I need, in Thee I find—
O Lamb of God, I come!

Just as I am Thou wilt receive,
Wilt welcome, pardon, cleanse, relieve,
Because Thy promise I believe—
O Lamb of God, I come!

Just as I am—Thy love unknown
Has broken every barrier down;
Now to be Thine, yea, Thine alone—
O Lamb of God, I come!

Just as I am—of that free love,
"The breadth, length, depth, and height" to prove,
Here for a season, then above—
O Lamb of God, I come!

The American William Bradbury and his colleague Thomas Hastings were responsible for the marriage of the text of "Just as I Am" to its long-familiar tune. Piano manufacturer, organist, choral conductor, composer, educator, and publisher, Bradbury was part of the cadre of enterprising young musicians whose efforts were then revolutionizing mid-nineteenth-century congregational song. The first printing of the text with its now common tune occurred in the mid-1860s in *Hallowed Songs*. In its American publication history, nearly 80 percent of printings since that time associate Bradbury's tune Woodworth with Elliott's text.

Dwight L. Moody, the foremost evangelist of the late nineteenth century, commended "Just as I Am" as the hymn that had "done the most good to the greatest number and has touched more lives helpfully than any other hymn." One of Elliott's clergyman brothers put it this way: "In the course of a long ministry I hope I have been permitted to see some fruit of my labours, but I feel that far more has been done by this single hymn of my sister."

Although "Just as I Am" was penned by a nineteenth-century Anglican, not all clergy of a much-changed twentieth-century Anglican Church welcomed its evangelical sentiments; Graham faced stiff opposition to his use of the invitation hymn during his early British crusades. Vocal critics—religious and secular—insisted that Graham's crusades manipulated people. American-style evangelism seemed to its British detractors emotional and flighty, a thing of the moment, lacking the beauty of ritual or the depth of mature spiritual awakening. In short, it was offensively un-British and un-Anglican.

As Graham's team planned their June 1966 crusade in Earl's Court, London, there was a raging press dispute over the authenticity of people's response to Graham's message: Was it manipulated or sincere? Did Graham rely on what the British press called "gimmickery techniques" like emotion-stirring hymns? Responding to this line of criticism, Graham decided to omit any use of "Just as I Am": "We are not going to have any singing, we are not going to have any organ playing," Barrows recalled Graham saying. "If you want to give your heart to Christ, come forward." On the first night without background music, one thousand people came. In the course of the next month, Graham preached to nearly one million people, with the services relayed to tens of thousands more in selected British cities. Earl's Court was his largest monthlong crusade to date, and some forty thousand attendees came forward to register decisions. In the end, Barrows recalled, "we did not have one invitation hymn or note sounded in Earl's Court." Every evening hundreds of inquirers made their way forward, clomping down the stairs and across the venue's wooden floors. The effect was unexpectedly powerful—and to some—unsettling. Years later Barrows reminisced that a few weeks into the meetings, journalists conceded the point and begged unsuccessfully for the return of "Just as I Am," now calling *the silence* "too emotional." Graham, however, was by then making his own statement. The noise of people making their way forward did not distract him, though others thought it awkward. In the end, press coverage of the Earl's Court meeting was largely favorable. The 1966 London campaign was the only time Barrows varied the crusade music ritual for the full length of a crusade. Otherwise, "Just as I Am" remained the iconic invitation hymn everywhere.

Charlotte Elliott's words were deeply personal, but from the day she wrote them, they had universal appeal. Pairing the lyrics with the "right" tune took three decades, but once the connection was cemented, the hymn took its place in Christianity around the globe. Its consistent use in a consistent style over six decades firmly associated it in the popular mind with Graham crusades. The song now appears in a wide variety of hymnals, and even where hymnals have fallen into disuse, the simple words and tune of "Just as I Am" still sound a familiar gospel call: "Come."

"How Great Thou Art"

A second song indelibly associated with the crusades came into the Graham team's repertoire in the mid-1950s. Barrows and Shea first encountered "How Great Thou Art" in London in 1954, introduced it to crusade audiences in Toronto in 1955, and from New York's Madison Square Garden in 1957, television carried it to the nation and then to the world.

As he walked down London's bustling Oxford Street on a March afternoon in 1954, Shea happened upon Andrew Gray, an acquaintance who managed the Glasgow-based Nonconformist (i.e., non-Anglican) publishing firm Pickering and Inglis, Ltd. Gray handed Shea a four-page leaflet that included what he called "a new hymn." The memorable three-month Billy Graham crusade at Harringay Arena was at its height, and people regularly suggested hymns they hoped would be used in crusade-related events. Shea noted in passing only that the "new hymn" appeared in two languages, Russian and English, and that it had a "strong" and "worshipful" English title, "How Great Thou Art," but otherwise he ignored it. Later that day, Barrows received a copy of the same leaflet, but he, too, put it aside. Shea sang 266 times during the twelve weeks of the Harringay crusade (singing a total of 125 separate songs), and his most popular numbers were "I'd Rather Have Jesus," "The Love of God," and "He's Got the Whole World in His Hands." Crusade songs—especially congregational numbers like "Blessed Assurance"—became "tube" or "bus" songs as crowds sang their way home, but the Harringay crusade ended without the singing of the suggested new hymn.

Months later, Barrows reviewed the new song and decided to introduce it at the fall 1955 Toronto crusade. Barrows, Shea, and pianist Tedd Smith worked out a simple arrangement for choir and Shea that was well received during the meetings. But the Toronto crusade was not broadcast, and the new hymn was simply one among many songs used to good effect. Not until Graham went to Manhattan's Madison Square Garden in 1957 did "How Great Thou Art" attain the prestige it would hold in Graham's ministry for the next fifty years.

By then, Shea and Barrows had learned that the hymn was not, in fact, new—although the English translation they had been given was fairly recent. "How Great Thou Art" had a long and convoluted history that illustrated how hymns often transcend cultures and languages, and the way lyrics could evolve considerably in the process of translation. The remarkable literary history of the hymn spanned seventy years and spoke into the stories of marginalized Protestants in Sweden, Germany, Russia, and eastern Europe—years before English missionary Stuart K. Hine undertook an English translation that became the basis of the hymn since sung around the globe. Like "Just as I Am," this song gained universal appeal and, thanks to the Graham crusades, quickly found a global audience.

The story of "How Great Thou Art" begins with Carl Gustav Boberg (1859-1940), a Swedish poet and politician from the picturesque town of Monsteras in coastal southeastern Sweden. Just off the shore, dozens of islands stretch into the Baltic Sea. The large island of Oland (now a UNESCO World Heritage Site) sheltered rare species and an early Paleolithic settlement. Life in the region was hard: rocky soil challenged farmers while the sea offered better, but riskier, opportunities. Strong religious currents swept through the village in both the eighteenth and nineteenth centuries as pietists in and outside the state church (Lutheran) in Boberg's native province of Kalmar made much of heartfelt faith and lively religion.

The son of a shipyard carpenter and a sometime sailor himself, Boberg embraced the warmhearted faith of the Lutheran pietists who associated with the Swedish Mission Covenant, a growing movement within the state church. Boberg attended the Mission Covenant's Bible school and returned to his home area as an evangelist. One day after a worship service in 1885, the beauty of the natural world around him—islands, sea, picture-perfect landscape—struck Boberg in a new way, and, as he contemplated creation, a thunderstorm blew in. Then, as distant church bells tolled, a rainbow stretched across the sky. In that setting—thrilled by a spectacular display of natural beauty—the twenty-six-year-old Boberg composed a nine-stanza hymn, "O Store Gud" ("O Great God").

Boberg's lines first appeared in print on March 13, 1886, in the small Monsteras paper. Set to a familiar Swedish folk tune, they were published next with words and instrumentation for piano and guitar in *Sannings-vittnet* ("The Witness of Truth"), a religious paper that Boberg edited. Eight stanzas were included in an 1890 Swedish Mission Covenant hymnal and quickly became a favorite within Mission Covenant circles. Boberg eventually sold the rights to the Mission Covenant, and all nine stanzas were printed in that association's 1891 hymnal set to an arrangement for voice, guitar, and piano by music teacher and organist Adolf Edgren. As members of the group migrated to the United States, they brought the song with them. An early English translation for use in the evolving Swedish American congregations was made in 1925 by the distinguished educator E. Gustav Johnson of the denomination's North Park College. He translated the text of "O Store Gud" along with twenty-two other Swedish hymns for inclusion in the Swedish Covenant Church hymnal (*Covenant Hymnal*, 1931):

> O mighty God, when I behold the wonder
> Of nature's beauty, wrought by words of thine,
> And how thou leadest all from realms up yonder
> Sustaining earthly life with love benign,
>
> REFRAIN
> With rapture filled, my soul thy name would laud,
> O mighty God! O mighty God!
> With rapture filled, my soul thy name would laud,
> O mighty God! O mighty God!

Estonia

Even as immigrants carried the song westward to America, pietist connections in the Baltic region gave it visibility to the east. Manfred von Glehn, an Estonian-born German nobleman whose family estates stretched along the Baltic Sea, heard the song among the Swedish diaspora in Estonia (then part of the Russian Empire). The Glehns belonged to a small, scattered German aristocracy that prospered far from their ancestral homeland. Wealthy and university educated, generations of the Glehns had been noted for their civic-mindedness. The family had recently been persuaded by Baptist evangelists to separate from the Lutheran church. Baptists, a much-ridiculed minority among German Protestants, attracted very few members of the Glehns' social class. The Glehn family's conversion occurred during a wave of spiritual renewal remembered in Estonia as the West Coast Revival. It swept across western Estonia in the 1870s and 1880s, flourishing first among Swedish pietist emigrants—Mission Covenant folk—and then among the German settlers when German Baptist itinerant preachers arrived. The Swedish hymn stirred hearts of the revived in all social classes, but predominantly in those of farmers and laborers.

And so, amid revival that established German Baptist congregations in Estonia and quickened Swedish pietist impulses in the same area, the aristocratic Glehns learned Boberg's Swedish pietist hymn, and Manfred von Glehn translated it into German, publishing six stanzas as "Du grosser Gott" in the *Blankenburger Lieder* in 1907. This publication venue assured the widest possible circulation among German Protestants of evangelical and pietist inclination. The hymnal was released in conjunction with the annual conferences in Blankenburg (in central Germany) of the Evangelical Alliance in Germany. Staunchly conservative sectarians despised the Evangelical Alliance for its emphasis on Christian unity, but Germans open to revival and in touch with proponents of renewal abroad embraced the new hymn and assisted its dissemination. In the wake of the disruption caused by World War I, Glehn's family migrated to Brazil in 1923. Before he left, though, a hymn that soon found its way into most German Protestant hymnals—state church and sectarian—assured his ongoing voice in German-speaking Protestantism.

Russia

Both the Swedish Mission Covenant and German Baptists in Estonia supported missionary work inside Russia. Situated as they were on the edges of the Russian Empire, they commissioned evangelists to penetrate Russia's cities as well as to press across vast open spaces into Siberia. These Swedish itinerants traveled nominally to work among Swedish sailors, German tradespeople, or other migrants, but the more daring reached out as well to the Russian Orthodox population. They also networked with a fast-growing number of Russian Protestants led largely by men who braved the constant threat of persecution. Among these was Ivan S. Prokhanov, sometimes called the "Martin Luther of Russia," who translated Glehn's "Du grosser Gott" into Russian as "Velikiy Bog" ("Great God") and published it in a Russian-language hymnal in St. Petersburg in 1912. Prokhanov had a remarkable command of languages and a first-class education in Russia and western Europe, and he did much to provide scattered Russian Protestants with hymnals, Bibles, and evangelistic literature.

A native of the Caucasus, Prokhanov was born in 1869 into a well-to-do family of Molokans ("milk people"), "spiritual Christians" who dissented from the Orthodox Church by prioritizing the Bible in matters of salvation, using milk products during Orthodox fasts, abstaining from pork, and rejecting icons and ornately appointed churches. Prokhanov came of age with a deep love for all things Russian but with an accompanying outrage at the inequities he saw around him. He had a particular passion for the plight of Christian minorities. In 1886, Prokhanov professed evangelical faith. On a cold Monday in January 1887, he was immersed in the icy waters of the River Terek and took as his motto "Life for Christ." In 1888, he enrolled in the Technical Institute at St. Petersburg after testing in the top 5 of 1,200 applicants for 200 openings.

Evangelical Christianity had begun gaining prominence in certain parts of Russia in the 1860s. In St. Petersburg, the wealthy Chertkov family invited such prominent British evangelicals as Lord Radstock to visit and explain what came to be known as "gospel Christianity." In Odessa, meanwhile, the mingling of German Lutheran and Mennonite settlers with the Russian population gave rise to an evangelical movement known as Stundism, from the German *Stunden*—or hours set aside for Bible reading and prayer. A third source of evangelical witness arose in the Caucasus region, Prokhanov's home territory, when several congregations of Molokans began systematic Bible study and took guidance from a German immigrant who happened to be a Baptist. The Molokans who followed him were baptized by immersion and took the name "Baptist." In 1884, representatives of these various evangelical movements gathered for a conference in St. Petersburg. Two days later the government intervened and banished some of its leaders. This harsh action was the first in a series of oppressive moves against Christian sectarians that followed the coronation of Czar Alexander III. Non-Orthodox Christians found it almost impossible to gather, and they had no legal standing. Eventually, all non-Orthodox religious services were outlawed, and all Protestant literature banned.

In St. Petersburg, Prokhanov forged Protestant connections and worked tirelessly to expand them among his fellow students. His religious work was primarily geared to private visitation and alleviation of suffering. After graduating, his life by day as an engineer was ordinary enough, but by night he studied his Bible, attended secret Christian meetings, and edited a small paper he hoped would encourage beleaguered Russian Protestants. When the secret police took up his trail, the American head of Westinghouse Air Brake Co. in St. Petersburg (who, with his family, also attended secret evangelical services) smuggled him out of the country. So began Prokhanov's connections in Finland, Sweden, Germany, France, and beyond.

Over the course of his life, Prokhanov did all he could to expand "gospel Christianity" in Russia. He traveled and studied abroad in the interests of evangelism at home and used his extraordinary gifts to nurture a growing church. Prokhanov translated, wrote, and published over 1,100 hymns; edited the main Russian-language evangelical periodical, *Khristianin* (the *Christian*), for twenty-two years; established the All-Russian Evangelical Christian Union in St. Petersburg (1909); evangelized, baptized, and encouraged prisoners; and eventually suffered imprisonment for the sake of his convictions.

A Russian hymnal was published despite government prohibition of all evangelical literature. In the absence of hymnals, most Russian Protestants used lyrics and, occasionally, musical notations written by hand. But the rapid growth of the evangelical movement created an urgent need for hymnals. Prokhanov compiled *Gusli* (*The Harps*) and in 1906 took the manuscript to a government printing plant that also accepted outside orders, asking for twenty thousand hymnals. The printer agreed, promised to deal with the censors, and completed the task in a few months. Prokhanov shipped them promptly, ever wary of censors and powerful Russian Orthodox opposition. An expanded edition, *Kimvali* (*The Cymbals*), was published in

1927. "Velikiy Bog/How Great Thou Art" (with eight stanzas) was the third hymn in this collection of 100 spiritual songs. It is likely that Prokhanov translated the text primarily from its German rendering while imprisoned by the Bolsheviks in 1921. His version appeared as well among 1,200-plus hymns published by the Baptist Kompas Press in Lodz, Poland.

Prokhanov's translation of "Du grosser Gott" mattered because of who he was: the one who traveled everywhere, preached, established a Bible school, published—or had a hand in publishing—most evangelical material in Russia, and was universally known throughout the dispersed Russian evangelical movement. When imprisoned, he evangelized prisoners; when at liberty, he resourced a growing number of "gospel Christians" in Russia. When Stalin barred his return from a fund-raising trip to Canada in 1925, some estimated that 4 million baptized Russian Protestants owed their conversions directly or indirectly to Ivan Stepanovich Prokhanov. In exile in Canada, he wrote his autobiography, a remarkable account of a little-known evangelistic effort under the shadow of czarist secret police and Communist hostility that changed the way millions of Russians lived. Those people—the marginalized and hunted Christians of an empire in turmoil and an evolving Marxist state—took comfort then and since in the majestic words of their own version of Carl Boberg's "How Great Thou Art."

Stuart Hine

The first English text for "O Mighty God" did not migrate outside of the North American Scandinavian immigrant community that used Gustav Johnson's 1925 translation. Rather, the popular English version known today derived from Prokhanov's Russian translation. Two English Open Brethren missionaries in southern Poland and northern Ukraine heard Prokhanov's translation from Glehn's German rendering of Boberg's Swedish text and made it their own. From 1923 until 1929, Stuart and Mercy Salmon Hine served near the Russian/Polish border, where they first heard "Velikiy Bog" soon after its publication in 1927. An Englishman born in 1899 and dedicated by his parents in a London Salvation Army unit into the "gospel war," Stuart Hine had professed faith under a gospel-singing evangelist named Madame Annie Ryall, an earnest pre–World War I British soul winner.

Soon after the war, Hine married Mercy Salmon, and within a month, the two departed for eastern Europe as Open Brethren missionaries. They arrived, they liked to recall, "with just a few coins and the rich promises of God." Their real goal was Russia, but after a few years in western Ukraine (some sources suggest that they left Ukraine during the Holomodor, Stalin's famine-genocide in the region), they settled in southern Poland, a few miles from the Russian border. There they mingled with Russians, traveled through the Carpathian Mountains, and began to evangelize, often singing as a duet Prokhanov's translation "Velikiy Bog." When the Hines' Polish residency permits were revoked, they resettled in Mukachevo, Ruthenia (Slovakia), where they remained until the outbreak of World War II forced them to return to England.

Stuart Hine's translation of "How Great Thou Art" from Russian to English emerged over time. He completed the first three stanzas after a 120-mile evangelistic mission by bicycle through the scenic Carpathian Mountains in 1934, where he heard "mighty thunder," rode through "woods and forest glades," and "heard birds sing sweetly in the trees." He distributed Gospels, sang and read Scripture in public squares, and talked to all who would listen. He recalled that the common English third stanza came to him after he entered a remote village, asked if any Protestants resided there, and followed directions to the home of a local laborer named Dimitri. Nineteen years earlier, a Russian soldier had left Dimitri a Bible, but no one in town could read it. Finally, Dimitri's wife learned to read and gathered her neighbors for Bible readings, and a small sectarian group was born. On approaching Dimitri's house, Hine overheard loud prayers of confession and adoration. He jotted down some of the phrases the congregation called out in prayer, and his musings turned into the following:

> And when I think that God, his Son not sparing
> Sent him to die, I scarce can take it in . . .
> Then sings my soul, my Savior, God, to thee,
> How great thou art! How great thou art!

Those words bore a striking similarity to the sixth stanza of Prokhanov's translation of the German, but Hine claimed different inspiration for penning them. On his return to Britain, Hine spent much of World War II evangelizing displaced Polish and Ukrainian refugees. During this period, he happened upon two professing Christians in a displaced persons camp. Their conversation about Christian hope, Hines said, inspired him to write the commonly used fourth stanza of "How Great Thou Art."

The wonder of redemption and the hope of heaven had been woven into the song in prior iterations. Hine, however, devoted a full stanza to each in what became the common third and fourth stanzas of the hymn, giving the topics greater prominence and otherwise substantially shortening the hymn. The translation of the hymn as it is generally known today was not completed until 1948.

After World War II, Hine wrote more hymns, edited hymnals, and published music. His version of "How Great Thou Art" first appeared in 1949 in *Grace and Peace*, a magazine he edited with the Russian diaspora in mind. Subscribers in fifteen countries thus had access to the hymn in two languages, and Hine accommodated requests for copies. He included his four-stanza "How Great Thou Art" in several other of his publications, and it began to find an audience among British Nonconformists whose missionaries took it abroad. People later recalled its use in the East African Revival and in Nagaland in India in the 1950s and '60s. Hine later claimed that it was first sung in the United States in 1951 by a Central American missionary attending a convention at the Stony Brook School in New York. Fuller Seminary scholar and revival promoter J. Edwin Orr heard a Naga tribal choir sing the hymn at Deolati, Bombay State, India. Deeply moved, Orr brought the song (as transcribed by a Mennonite missionary) to a college conference at the Forest Home Christian Conference Center in Southern California in 1954. Orr knew nothing of the song's history and handed it on to Cyrus Nettleton Nelson of Gospel Light Publications, who copyrighted it with minor changes later in 1954. Gospel Light published it in the form of broadsides. Thanks to its use at Forest Home, the song also reached Manna Music founder Tim Spencer, who later obtained publishing rights directly from Hine. And so, when Hine's translation came into the hands of Shea and Barrows, it was as if the song's time had come.

Crusade Theme

However faithfully one charts the history and occasional earlier uses of Hine's translation, it is abundantly evident that Barrows's selection of the hymn for the 1957 Madison Square Garden Billy Graham crusade made the song known and loved across denominations and around the globe. Its use in English before 1957 had been limited. In the 1957 crusade, Shea—backed by a mass choir and in response to popular demand—sang the song 100 times as, for the first time, television beamed a few of the services nationwide. From 1957 on, Barrows never omitted multiple renderings of "How Great Thou Art" from any crusade, and the song came to function as the de facto crusade theme song. Graham personally urged its use and shared his thoughts with Hine. "The reason I like 'How Great Thou Art,'" he wrote, "is because it glorifies God: it turns a Christian's eyes toward God rather than upon himself, as so many songs do. I did something I rarely do—I urged Cliff Barrows to use it as often as possible, because it was such a God-honoring song."

The first time Shea sang "How Great Thou Art" in New York, he made two slight alterations to Hine's first stanza: "mighty thunder" became "rolling thunder," and "consider all the works thy hands have made" became "consider all the worlds thy hands have made." Shea did not inform Barrows in advance, and Barrows recalled the twinkle and smile Shea sent in his direction when he noticed. Given the growing impact of the new "space race," the change from "works" to "worlds" captured the mood of the moment in the West. Shea's alterations became the preferred American version, and when Manna Music negotiated with Hine for rights to the international copyright, they published the song with Shea's wording.

The song was an instant hit at the New York crusade and made an impression upon both audiences and observers alike. In early September, a reporter for the *New York Times* ventured to say that "many persons attending the Graham rallies in the Garden were moved more by Mr. Shea's rendering of 'How Great Thou Art' than by the preaching of the evangelist." The song became so popular that the New York Crusade Office distributed a souvenir paper and plastic 78 rpm record to all who wrote in response to televised broadcasts of the crusade. The office called these "talking pictures," and they were designed to be played on a record player or mounted on a wall. The picture featured Madison Square Garden, Shea, and the crusade choir; the "talking" part was the choir's performance of "How Great Thou Art."

Years later, Shea recalled arriving in his room one night in the middle of the 1957 crusade only to wonder if he had sung "How Great Thou

Art." The moment stayed with him for the rest of his life, because to him it represented the danger of singing a hymn because it was on the program rather than singing to engage in thoughtful ministry. As he told it, he resolved never to let such a thing happen again: each song would be sung with awareness of the ministry-of-the-moment.

Shea also resolved to reserve "How Great Thou Art" a special place in his repertoire. As he walked the streets of cities around the world, people often recognized him and asked for a song. He refused requests for "How Great Thou Art" because he regarded it as a hymn of adoration suited especially to worship rather than as a song to entertain. Shea's last solo in Graham's final crusade, New York 2005, was "How Great Thou Art."

Certainly "How Great Thou Art" topped the list of Graham crusade favorites for several reasons: its message of God's creative and redemptive power; its arrangement for Shea and mass choir; audience response; media. Shea's strong voice backed by a mass choir contributed as well to the popularity of the song. Audiences associated it with him, and popular demand made it feature in every crusade. Once it became a regular at Graham crusades—and once Graham crusades were routinely broadcast—"How Great Thou Art" took America by storm. Within a decade, Elvis Presley had won his first Grammy for the hymn, sung with Shea's minor alterations. A long, diverse list of artists have covered the song over the years, including Mahalia Jackson, Burl Ives, Pat Boone, Tennessee Ernie Ford, Cliff Richard, Dolly Parton, and Carrie Underwood. The hymn soon took its place in a wide variety of American hymnals, Protestant and Catholic, mainline and evangelical, generally with Shea's variations. The Mormon Tabernacle Choir recorded its own stunning arrangement for choir and orchestra. Like "Amazing Grace," "How Great Thou Art" found a place in the larger American culture. Lawrence Welk claimed in the 1960s that it was the most requested sacred or secular song on his celebrated variety show (then rated the most popular show of all time). In 1978, the American Society of Composers, Artists, and Publishers named it "The All-Time Outstanding Gospel Song in America." In 1994—in recognition that "How Great Thou Art" often topped lists of Americans' favorite hymns— the Gospel Music Association inducted Stuart K. Hine (posthumously) into its hall of fame. And in March 2001, the National Endowment of the Arts and the Recording Industry Association of America ranked Shea's 1955 recording number 204 in its list of the 365 most important recordings of the twentieth century.

Disagreements

While "How Great Thou Art" became spectacularly popular because of its central role in Graham's crusades and quickly moved into a preeminent place within the canon of American hymnody, one person was apparently unhappy about the song's route to success: Stuart Hine. In 1967 Hine wrote a letter to Graham, accusing the team of altering text and music. Correspondence included an undercurrent of unhappiness over royalty arrangements—royalties to which Hine thought he was entitled. Like many other things, dealing with Hine became Barrows's responsibility, and their exchanges became so fraught that Barrows finally admitted that, had he had any inkling of Hine's petulance and the distress the crusade use of the hymn would cause, he might never have introduced the song at all. At the same time, though, he admitted that the song was worth the "travail."

Barrows's office handled all crusade music copyright and permission arrangements, and he scrupulously followed every requirement. In reality, Hine's root problem was actually with the copyright arrangements he had first leased to Manna Music, rather than with the Graham team. Barrows obtained the requisite permissions from Manna, but the sheer magnitude of Graham's reach fueled Hine's fury. There simply was no way to compete. Hine professed to want no money but then complained that he was subsidizing the copies the BGEA freely distributed in the United States. The Graham organization actually made no money on the hymn; rather, as Barrows put it in a 1968 letter to Hine, the BGEA merely wanted "to share around the world the inspiration and blessing of [the hymn's] use." Barrows further assured Hine that the Graham team did not resent any royalties Hine received. For them, Barrows insisted, it was a matter of ministry, not money. Frustrated, Hine began enumerating further grievances.

Hine now claimed that Shea's word change of "works" to "worlds" fundamentally altered the message of the song, since Hine had intended "works" to include Christ's work of redemption. The Graham team's decision to offload (free of charge) in Britain several thousand extra copies of *Crusader Hymns and Hymn Stories*, a book prepared for distribution in the

United States to people who wrote in to the BGEA, aggravated copyright problems. *Crusader Hymns* used Shea's wording for "How Great Thou Art," and Hine insisted that he owned the copyright for all British use: therefore, *Crusader Hymns* could not circulate in England without also including his text. He grumbled that *Crusader Hymns* included such American favorites as "The Battle Hymn of the Republic," and even suggested that it was treasonable to circulate in Britain a book including an American patriotic song that meanwhile omitted "God Save the Queen." When demand for the book in Britain grew, the BGEA printed a second run in Britain, a prudent decision considering the cost of shipping. But Hine was livid: he had grudgingly accepted the book's publication in the United States, but republishing the same text in Britain violated his rights, he insisted, and he made even louder noises about treason. Hine also demanded that Manna Music print the "correct" version of "How Great Thou Art" alongside every printing of the Graham crusades' "distorted" lyrics. "The BGEA caused confusion by bursting into my [Hine's] British and Australian markets without the slightest warning to me," he grumbled.

All of Barrows's attempts to appease Hine failed. Hine became ever more rancorous, and both sides turned the matter over to lawyers. Meanwhile, certain that their use of the hymn conformed to legal requirements, Barrows persisted in featuring what had quickly become a much-demanded crusade favorite in many languages. The Billy Graham crusade version of the song—recorded many times by Shea and a long list of music notables, religious and secular—popularized the slightly adapted American version of Hine's translation until it became the standard in much of the world. The power of media and the magnitude of Graham's influence made that result a foregone conclusion.

And so, two songs, indelibly associated with crusades, became hallmarks of the Graham enterprise but also classic Christian hymns sung everywhere Christians worshiped. For "Just as I Am," popularity was not new, but the Graham crusades modeled actions that suited the words. "Coming" became more than an inner choice: it was an inner choice with consequences in public action. Though its private dimension remained essential, rising, walking forward, receiving counseling, and enrolling in follow-up activities as the song was sung made people "own" their decision in a way that made them accountable. "How Great Thou Art" concentrated focus on divine redemption and was easily the most popular choir/Shea number in every crusade around the globe.

These two songs took pride of place among the songs performed by the choir and Shea. Their counterparts for congregational singing were Crosby's "Blessed Assurance" and "To God Be the Glory." However, over the years a third element of crusade music quickly began to share the spotlight. While Shea and mass choirs featured prominently from the first crusades onward, audiences increasingly also warmed to a growing group of regular and special crusade guests—"many voices" who sang the "one song" with their own diverse stylistic, regional, and ethnic variations.

6

GUEST VOICES

I sing because I'm happy;
I sing because I'm free;
For his eye is on the sparrow,
And I know he watches me.

—"His Eye Is on the Sparrow," Civilla Martin, 1905

f crusade music combined the older, newer, classical, and innovative, how was it selected? Beyond running each decision through the litmus test of their nonnegotiable principles, how did Barrows and Shea choose instrumentalists, vocalists, songs? The friendship networks that sufficed in the first year or two soon needed to be supplemented. The length and scope of crusades grew too fast to rely on the goodwill of otherwise-engaged radio partners or the long-term availability of acquaintances. Given the incessant demands on an inexperienced team, the organizational form of the BGEA and its musical framework and procedures took shape with amazing rapidity and surprising efficiency. Fortunately, the Graham team had at its disposal individuals—either as consultants or staff—trained by earlier evangelists (notably Billy Sunday) who stood ready to pitch in and put their experience to good use.

One way of thinking about crusade music is to recognize that it consti-tuted a reflection of the crusade's overall theme. Whatever was going to be said, emphasized, or refuted had its musical counterpart, and whatever music was used served literary, theological, and evangelistic purposes. Barrows headed the list of decision makers. He had a core list of crusade songs from which he drew, giving the campaigns both a common message and sound. The early crusade hymnals he prepared provided a common source on which to draw—and provided the core of what future crusade hymnals might contain. For the most part, local crusade planners expressed a desire for the "standard" crusade sound and were satisfied to have Barrows take the lead in selection. He, however, routinely solicited input from local leaders, especially when crusades were held abroad. At issue, too, were what selections would be featured in targeted overseas editions of *The Hour of Decision* in the months leading up to a foreign crusade. The radio broadcast sometimes aired only around crusades, and linking the music offered one simple way to tie crusade services into the larger evangelistic enterprise.

Committees and detailed handbooks stood at the core of the crusade musical experience. Committees were organized on the local and the regional levels and enjoyed different degrees of responsibility, from recruiting choir members and recommending guest artists to selecting music, arranging rehearsals, and integrating the activities of choirs numbering five thousand and more. Barrows's office took responsibility for acquiring copies and copyrights and for moving music to destinations in time for rehearsals and services. Barrows also tackled the process of identifying satisfactory local guest artists. For larger services, he often brought a few artists from abroad or relied on several who had served with distinction before. For regional rallies, he sometimes turned to recommended local talent that was readily available and had a good local draw. Because for the most part crusade music remained anchored in the sounds of mass choirs, Shea, and one other familiar performer—often an African American singer like Myrtle Hall or Ethel Waters—there was not much room in a schedule for more performers from abroad. One or two generally sufficed. This coincided with local wishes. Everywhere crowds mobbed venues for precrusade concerts with Shea, his accompanist Tedd Smith, and one or another of his American vocalist colleagues.

Barrows made an effort to discover which Christian songs were popular in each crusade locale. Questionnaires and surveys assessed the usefulness of particular songs and the attitude of choir members toward their impact. Barrows employed translators when needed and used music to help local audiences "own" the crusade. In some places, he found the task easy. In South Korea, for example, missionary translations of American gospel songs were in common use, and so a familiar idiom stood ready for appropriation. In Germany, on the other hand, Protestants were divided over what to use, which translations were best, or who might be the official "connection" to the Graham association. In the end, this curtailed some musical opportunities.

North American crusades presented a different challenge as years went by, as Barrows, son of California's already diverse landscape, attempted to identify performers whose musical idiom would speak to regional and national cultural, ethnic, and racial diversity. As we have already seen, in the team's very early years this diversity came first in the form of singers like Stuart Hamblen and Redd Harper, whose popular, country-tinged "cowboy" sounds scandalized some staid northern Protestants but moved the needle with audiences hailing from southern cultural origins. Down through the years singers representing this—broadly speaking, "country"—cultural base provided a steady flow of guest artists for the crusades through performers like Johnny Cash (see below), Glen Campbell, Randy Travis, Barbara Mandrell, and Ricky Skaggs.

But the Graham sound also would include a more targeted appeal to distinct European American "ethnic" audiences. For instance, Chicago's Italian American Palermo Brothers ("'At'sa Louie, Im'a Phil!"), old YFC favorites, were frequent platform guests over the years. During the 1960s and 1970s, artists hailing from non-WASP immigrant enclaves within the larger evangelical subculture were also frequently represented via such artists as Norma (Larsen) Zimmer, Evie Tornquist (Norwegian American), and Ken Medema (Dutch American).

During the 1960s, Barrows and the larger Graham organization realized that the changes and progress represented by the growing civil rights movement demanded more purposeful attempts to give exposure for black voices within Graham's ministry. Part of this effort included bringing black preachers like Howard Jones and Ralph Bell onboard as associate evangelists. Likewise, incorporating African American musical artists became an important means of establishing the message that the crusades were meant for all Americans. In addition to early appearances by African American church choirs and artists like Mahalia Jackson and Ethel Waters (see below), a number of new black voices were added to the crusade mix beginning in the mid-1960s. One frequent contributor was Myrtle Hall, who made her first appearance in 1966 at the Southern Piedmont Crusade (Greenville, South Carolina); Hall would be featured on crusade platforms for the following twenty-five years. A number of other African American artists, representing a wide spectrum of musical styles and genres, repeatedly enriched the crusades' music program in the following decades, including Willa Mae Dorsey, Kathleen Battle, Andraé Crouch, Larnelle Harris, Babbie Mason, the Dannibelles, Deniece Williams, Johnny Ray Watson, Leontyne Price, Jessy Dixon, CeCe Winans, Joe Bias, and Nicole C. Mullen. In seeking out black musical partners for the Graham ministry, Barrows made an important statement about the BGEA's vision to the American public, while providing the artists with access to vast new publics.

A similar strategy and impact occurred in terms of Barrows's utilization of newer minority voices. As the BGEA's ministry broadened and the realization took hold that North America's ethnic mosaic was growing ever more diverse, Barrows and his music committee eagerly sought out a wider representation of performers that reflected the face of America. This meant frequent appearances by artists like the Hawaiians (Mark and Diane Yasuhara), the Katinas (a Samoan American brothers and sister group), Susan Aglukark (Inuit), and Korean American sopranos Kim Wickes and Sung Sook Lee. Particularly noticeable—given the growth of America's Latino/a population—was the growing participation of Hispanic performers, including solo artists such as Manuel Bonilla, Pablo Hinojos, Jaci Velasquez, and Fernando Ortega, as well as groups like Salvador (winner of a 2003 Dove Award) and the New Mexico–based band Los Blue Ventures de Louis Sanchez. Barrows deemed music one way to be inclusive, and over the years he increasingly used it at every turn.

As these lists of performers show, celebrity artists played a prominent role in crusade music from the outset—even if they were only celebrities for a night. Born-again Miss America candidates rehearsed special numbers and sang solos at crusades, as did local bands or contest winners. Locally known singers and talent-show winners warmed up the crowds during the meetings. In the process, different as each might be, they conformed to the theological and spiritual requirements of singing "one song." Barrows made sure of that, and he sought to enlist every guest artist as an integral team member for each particular service in which the artist participated.

Fanny Crosby (Alpha Historica / Alamy Stock Photo)

"Amazing Grace" sheet music (BGEA)

"Ivory Palaces" sheet music (BGEA)

Tedd Smith (seated at piano) and George Beverly Shea (BGEA)

Tedd Smith, Cliff Barrows, and George Beverly Shea (BGEA)

George Beverly Shea at
ABC microphone (BGEA)

George Beverly Shea with "I'd Rather Have Jesus" music in background (BGEA)

Roy Rogers on his horse Trigger at a special rally for children at Harringay Stadium, London, March 3, 1954 (Keystone Pictures / ZUMAPRESS / Newscom)

Roy Rogers and Billy Graham (BGEA)

Billy Graham, Ruth Graham, Dale Evans, and Roy Rogers
(UPPA / Photoshot / Newscom)

Ethel Waters at a Billy Graham crusade with Cliff Barrows directing the choir (BGEA)

Billy Graham and Ethel Waters (BGEA)

Johnny Cash and Billy Graham backstage during 1974 Norfolk crusade (BGEA)

Billy Graham and Bill Gaither during 2001 Louisville crusade (BGEA)

Cliff Barrows, Billy Graham, and George Beverly Shea singing at 1984 Sunderland, England, crusade (BGEA)

Billy Graham at Miami Rock Festival, December 28, 1969 (AP Photo / Robert Houston)

Billy Graham choir in Puerto Rico, March 16, 1995 (AP Photo / John McConnic)

Cliff Barrows directing the choir during a Billy Graham crusade (BGEA)

dc Talk onstage during 1994 Cleveland crusade (BGEA)

Billy Graham praying with dc Talk during 1994 Cleveland crusade (BGEA)

Billy Graham (seated in pulpit) speaking to the 80,000 people at the Greater New York Billy Graham Crusade at Flushing Meadows, Corona Park, in New York, June 25, 2005 (Todd Sumlin / KRT / Newscom)

George Beverly Shea and Cliff Barrows speaking at the ceremony for the library dedication service for Billy Graham that took place in his hometown of Charlotte, NC, May 31, 2007 (Jason Moore / ZUMA Press / Newscom)

George Beverly Shea and Billy Graham (BGEA)

He, Shea, Tedd Smith, and a changing cast of organists constituted the unchanging center that governed text, tune, and performance style. Nonetheless, Barrows, Shea, and the musical team realized that the crusades benefited immensely from the opportunity to draw upon wildly popular entertainers whose forthright Christian testimonies swelled crowds.

Stuart Hamblen's conversion during Graham's first crusade in Los Angeles had suggested a new range of possibilities. The sensation Hamblen's testimony created as well as his very public lifestyle changes showed the appeal of a secular star, especially one whose testimony had links to crusade ministry. As soon as the Los Angeles crusade concluded, Hamblen began traveling the YFC circuit and singing his song, "It Is No Secret What God Can Do." He remained a popular broadcaster and crooner with an established public and continued to produce new songs. When he appeared as an advertised guest on a crusade platform, people were drawn to hear him in person and purchase his records. Hamblen, in turn, measurably increased the audience that experienced the regular crusade ritual orchestrated by Barrows, Shea, and Graham.

One of the next crusade sensations also came to Graham's attention through the Hollywood Christian Group, first appearing on a crusade platform at London's Harringay Arena in March 1954. Roy Rogers and Dale Evans had recently publicly professed Christian faith, and Graham gladly welcomed them to his platforms. By the mid-1950s, Rogers had starred in dozens of Hollywood westerns (he would eventually tally more than a hundred) and regularly appeared on the top-ten list of money-making western actors. A recording artist with Decca Records and founding member of the popular music ensemble the Sons of the Pioneers, Rogers also had millions of radio and television followers who tuned in weekly to *The Roy Rogers Show*. Hit songs like "Tumbling Tumbleweed," "Here Comes Peter Cottontail," and "Money Can't Buy Love" sold millions of records. His costar and wife, Dale Evans, counted her own list of Hollywood feature film credits (beginning opposite John Wayne in *In Old Oklahoma*, 1943), as well as a growing number of popular songs—including "Happy Trails to You," Evans's hit theme song on *The Roy Rogers Show*. The couple's annual rodeo at Madison Square Garden set box-office records. The Rogerses endorsed hundreds of products, from cereals to wristwatches, cap guns, and paper dolls. Their names and images were ubiquitous.

Rogers and Evans also enjoyed spectacular success on the other side of the Atlantic when Graham stepped to the platform to introduce them to an overflow crowd. Television, radio, comic books, and movies had won the King of the Cowboys and the Queen of the West hundreds of thousands of fans in the United Kingdom—their fan club in London alone counted some fifty thousand members. The British public proved eager to hear from these icons of American film and television, and in 1954 their clear testimonies and western-inspired songs brought a new sound to a crusade. (Also present at Harringay was cowboy singer Redd Harper, another recent convert of the Hollywood Christian Group. Fittingly, Henrietta Mears made an appearance, too.)

Rogers and Evans sat on the Harringay platform during several gloomy mid-March evenings supporting Graham's efforts and delighting crowds with upbeat testimonies and their splendid western dress until, at the end of the week, the special moment their young fans awaited finally arrived. It happened early on a Saturday afternoon in a dog-racing track adjacent to Harringay Arena when Rogers and Evans—accompanied by Rogers's famous golden palomino Trigger ("the Smartest Horse in the Movies")—put on a western show for London children. The event was free, but no adult was permitted past the gate without a child in tow. The couple wove testimony and song into a typical western routine, thrilling an overflow audience that exceeded forty thousand. They concluded with an invitation to a special afternoon Graham rally at Harringay.

The Rogerses had arranged their British tour through Ireland, England, and Scotland in conversation with Graham, and their bookings brought them to London as the crusade gained momentum. Wherever they had stopped en route, crowds jammed streets to glimpse Evans in her fringes, satins, and studs and Rogers in his trademark white Stetson and silver-tipped boots putting the world's most famous horse through its paces. Rogers, Evans, and Trigger had been a smash hit from the start. Trigger even carried Rogers's suitcase up hotel staircases and appeared in London on Rogers's hotel balcony before being led off to a stable. The crusade could not have purchased better advertising than the free public sightings of Rogers, Evans, and Trigger.

In their recent journey toward faith, Rogers and Evans had interacted with some of the same people whose example influenced Stuart and Suzy

Hamblen. Evans renewed a childhood profession of faith shortly after she married Rogers in 1947. The daughter of devout Southern Baptists, Evans (her given name was Frances Octavia Smith) spent her formative years in rural Texas and Arkansas attending church, Sunday school, and the Baptist Young People's Union. She made a childhood profession of faith but rebelled as a young teenager. Married at fourteen and divorced at sixteen with responsibility for an infant son, she married twice more before her big stage and music breaks came in Hollywood in the early 1940s. Meanwhile, her parents reared their grandson in the faith their daughter spurned. When a teenaged Tom Fox joined his mother in Hollywood, he found a welcome at Fountain Avenue Baptist Church. The pastor was John ("Jack") MacArthur, host of the *Voice of Calvary* broadcast (and father of John MacArthur, pastor of Grace Community Church in Sun Valley and founder of The Master's Seminary). He had honed his passion for evangelism under Charles E. Fuller of *Old-Fashioned Revival Hour* fame, and he took an interest in the spiritual well-being of Tom Fox's famous mother. As Evans's relationship with Rogers (by then her costar in several popular movies) headed toward marriage—her fourth, his third—Fox confronted his mother about her need for a vital faith. Preparing to get married himself, he told Evans that her marriage to Rogers would be another failure unless she had "a personal relationship with Jesus Christ." Evans and Rogers married on Wednesday, December 31, 1947. A few months later, Evans attended a Sunday evening service with her son. When Fox urged her to respond to MacArthur's message, Evans angrily refused. By the next Sunday, however, she yielded to the invitation. Shortly afterward, she began singing on MacArthur's broadcast and urging Rogers and his children to accompany her to church.

Like Evans, Rogers (born Leonard Slye and raised in southern Ohio) came from a Protestant family, but unlike his wife, he had never personally professed Christian faith. Evans began taking Rogers's three children to church, and he soon joined the family in the pews of Fountain Avenue Baptist. He found in MacArthur a mentor who answered his questions, kept his confidences, and refused to use Rogers and Evans for his own benefit. Rogers did not walk the church aisle as Evans had done: he committed his life to Christ after a Saturday evening cocktail party at his home where he had convened his friends to celebrate his latest movie. The next night he attended church. He gave his first public testimony to faith at the Forest Home Conference Center, and on Palm Sunday, March 21, 1948, MacArthur baptized Rogers and his daughter Cheryl on profession of faith.

From 1954 onward, Roy Rogers and Dale Evans appeared often at Graham crusades alone or together. As he aged, Rogers remained "everybody's image of a cowboy." His *Los Angeles Times* obituary called him the personification of a myth he helped create "of a West that never was." Through his long career he portrayed honesty, virtue, kindness, and decency that always triumphed. The film industry honored him with three stars on the Hollywood Walk of Fame; Dale Evans earned two. While Rogers preferred singing to speaking at crusades, Evans spoke freely, admitting that part of her longed to be an evangelist. "But," she continued, "I think God has revealed to me that I can serve him best by just remaining at my post."

Three years after Rogers and Evans began augmenting and delighting crusade crowds, the Graham team undertook its first crusade in New York City. On Thursday evening, July 25, 1957, after a sweltering day, nearly seventeen thousand people crammed into the air-conditioned comfort of Madison Square Garden to hear Graham preach on finding peace with God. The audience was a mere fraction of the one hundred thousand who had braved the suffocating heat wave at a Graham rally in Yankee Stadium a few days earlier, but in this more intimate setting, the crowd was treated to a crusade "first"—a solo from the legendary African American actress and jazz and blues singer Ethel Waters. By request, Waters sang the early twentieth-century gospel song "His Eye Is on the Sparrow"—"her" song— from her recent role in the stage and movie versions of Carson McCullers's novel *Member of the Wedding*. That evening Waters became the first of a long line of African American crusade soloists. When she faced the crowd in 1957, she was several years past the peak of her pioneering performance career. She had made and lost several fortunes, and the days when *Life* magazine called her "America's No. 1 Negro actress" seemed a distant memory.

Waters's presence at a Graham crusade that July evening came about in an unexpected way. Each Monday, Wednesday, and Friday, Waters appeared live on *Meet Tex and Jinx*, a hugely popular early radio talk show on New York's WEAF featuring John Reagan "Tex" McCrary and his wife, Eugenia Lincoln "Jinx" Falkenburg. The Graham crusade opened on

Wednesday, May 15, and in preparation, McCrary interviewed Ruth Graham. The day after Ruth's appearance, McCrary abruptly asked Waters on air if she thought the crusade would succeed. She replied, "Yes," and McCrary asked "Why?" Waters's response, "Because God don't sponsor no flops," was reported to the Graham team's New York office. Associate evangelist Lane Adams—charged with connecting the crusade to New York's entertainers—called to offer the singer tickets, promising that she could avoid the lines and have a guaranteed seat. She accepted a week's supply and attended, she said, to "see if [Graham] was for real" and "to do a little light criticizing." Waters was estranged from the church and had not attended a service, wedding, or funeral for nearly fifty years (though she had previously tuned into Graham's radio broadcast, *The Hour of Decision*), but each night at the crusade Graham seemed to speak directly to her spiritual needs. She became convinced that her alienation from God was not God's fault but her own. When the week ended, Waters called the crusade office to request more tickets. The secretary suggested that she sign on as a counselor or choir member. Waters opted for the choir but insisted that no one acknowledge her presence.

The next challenge was finding a choir seat. Waters weighed some three hundred pounds, and the choir seats had rigid sides. When Barrows arrived early to check on arrangements for the next evening's service, he noticed an assistant walking through the choir section shaking chairs. The man told Barrows he was looking for a seat with a loose left armrest. He found one on the second-row aisle in the alto section, removed the armrest, and that night Waters joined the choir.

For the first two months, her anonymity held. Barrows knew who she was but respected her wish and never spoke to, or of, her. During this time under Graham's preaching, Waters renewed her childhood Christian commitment. Public response led Graham's team to extend the crusade, and, during a choir rehearsal in July, Barrows finally broke his silence and surprised Waters by inviting her to sing "His Eye Is on the Sparrow" with choir backup. She bowed her assent, and the choir erupted in applause. That evening Waters began meeting the Graham platform team, and a few days later, she stepped out from the choir to solo. Waters was eager. She had counted the cost to her entertainment career and opted to identify publicly with the message Graham preached. For the remaining twenty years of her life, Graham crusades resurrected her career and brought her a different public. Waters could often be found singing the gospel at Graham crusades, generally "His Eye Is on the Sparrow," a song she marked out as her own (and objected to others singing). In time she added other numbers like her own "Partner with God," "Precious Lord," and a variation on "Oh, How I Love Jesus."

Waters's best-known song came from the pen of Civilla Durfee Martin, a Canadian who married Walter Stillman Martin, a Harvard-educated American pastor. Martin wrote several poems that became popular hymns (such as "God Will Take Care of You"), some of them set to tunes by her husband. The inspiration for "His Eye Is on the Sparrow" came to Martin in 1905 during a conversation with physically challenged friends in Elmira, New York, who expressed cheerful confidence in God's care. The prolific hymn writer Charles Gabriel ("Send the Light," "I Stand Amazed in the Presence") provided a tune, and the song was published in 1905.

In the crusades, Waters came to be known for her broad smile and warm manner, but her life began in troubled circumstances. Born in Chester, Pennsylvania, in 1896, the daughter of a teenaged rape victim, Waters would later say: "No one raised me. I just ran wild." At the age of twelve, Waters professed Christian faith, but soon thereafter, another youth at the church attacked her physically in the church lobby. Waters gave up church for good: she knew that Christianity required her to forgive her attacker, and she simply could not. Married as a young teen, she soon left an abusive relationship to support herself as a hotel maid.

At seventeen Waters began an entertainment career that took her quickly from bars to Broadway. She began singing in a Philadelphia club, moved on to Baltimore, and then traveled the vaudeville circuit as Sweet Mama Stringbean. Waters came to be known for her versatility, singing blues, jazz, big band, and pop tunes in clubs and theaters around the country.

A celebrated figure in the Harlem Renaissance, she sang in the 1920s at the Plantation Club. After recording first with a few smaller labels (beginning with the black label Black Swan in 1921), Waters signed with Columbia Records in 1925. She was featured regularly on radio shows and recorded hit versions of some of her era's most popular songs: "Dinah," "Stormy Weather," "I'm Coming Virginia," "Cabin in the Sky," "Am I Blue?" and "Taking a Chance."

Her first Broadway run (of a dozen) came in the 1920s, and her first Hollywood role (of nine) followed a decade later. During the 1930s, she performed at New York's Cotton Club, where she made "Stormy Weather" her signature song. Irving Berlin heard her there in 1933 and signed her for her first major Broadway triumph, *As Thousands Cheer*. Berlin gave Waters equal billing with the prominent white performers in his critically acclaimed revue. Early critics said things like "Ethel Waters knows how to make a song stand on tiptoe." Waters later professed to prefer acting to singing, but singing established her reputation.

In 1940 she won critical acclaim in the movie version of the musical *Cabin in the Sky*. The second African American woman nominated for an Academy Award (Best Supporting Actress for *Pinky*, 1949), she was the first black woman nominated for a Grammy and the first to play the lead role in a network television series (*Beulah*, ABC, 1950-1953). Her stage performance in *Member of the Wedding* won her the New York Drama Critics Circle Award in 1950.

After her association with Graham rekindled her faith, Waters could often be found in the alto section of crusade choirs on the nights she did not solo. She contributed her talent, and in return she found in Graham's core team a family that cared about her troubles, whether with the IRS, her health, or loneliness. After 1957, Waters made guest appearances on various shows and starred in the Graham film *The Heart of a Rebel* (World Wide Pictures, 1958—which had the New York City crusade as a backdrop), but declining strength gradually curtailed her activities.

In 1972, Billy and Ruth Graham hosted a tribute dinner for Waters at the Century Plaza Hotel in Los Angeles. Television personality Hugh Downs served as master of ceremonies, and the program featured a mix of her friends from the entertainment industry and her more recent religious work. Waters—accompanied by a New York stage musician—sang a selection of her hit songs. Bob Hope spoke words of appreciation. President Nixon sent a recorded message, and Tricia Nixon Cox brought his personal greetings. Then crusade pianist Tedd Smith moved to the piano, Billy Graham came to the podium, and Cliff Barrows presented an award. At Graham's bidding, Waters concluded the evening with her testimony and led the crowd in "His Eye Is on the Sparrow."

Difficulties hounded Waters to her end—multiple physical problems, poverty, loneliness. Nonetheless, until a year before her death in 1977, Waters gave Graham crusades priority in her schedule. When Graham learned of her passing, he shared words from their last conversation: "I'm sitting on the edge of Heaven, and he still has his eye on me."

Waters proved a strong addition to crusade music. Her pleasing personality, broad smile, and uninhibited style exuded her delight in her role and her love for Graham's team. The only artist to refer to the team as "her boys" and to Graham as "her baby Billy," Waters brought the variety the public associated with a skilled African American performer to Graham's stage. At about the same time Waters sang her first crusade solo, another singer was beginning to make his own mark in the world of popular music. Just over a decade later, Johnny Cash would make the first of many appearances at a Graham crusade.

"Country sweeps the country," wrote Goddard Lieberman in the *New York Times* in July 1957. Lieberman, the president of Columbia Records, had a front-row seat from which to view the nation's evolving taste in music. Coinciding with the growing migration of southern whites, which had begun during the Depression, accelerated during World War II, and continued to gain momentum in the 1950s, recent record sales revealed— much to the surprise of northern urban elites—a ravenous national appetite for music from the South. Billed as "the simple music of the common people," country came in a variety of styles, drawing from pop, traditional folk music, bluegrass, cowboy tunes, and the blues. A string of smash hits by a young Arkansan named Johnny Cash—"Hey, Porter," "I Walk the Line," and "Folsom Prison Blues," among others—highlighted the range of country music's influences and marked the young singer's phenomenal rise to the top of the charts. "I Walk the Line" reached number one on the *Billboard* country charts, and number seventeen on *Billboard*'s "Hot 100." Cash quickly became the number one artist for Memphis's Sun Records, the label that a few years earlier had discovered Elvis Presley.

In April 1959, Cash took a break from his relentless American tour schedule to accept a jam-packed week of engagements in Australia and Tasmania. Billed by his hosts as the "King of Western Rock-n-Roll," Cash and his sidekicks, the Tennessee Three (Luther Perkins, Marshall Grant, and W. S. Holland), along with several other performers, booked back-to-back appearances in Melbourne, Hobart, Sydney, Brisbane, and Newcastle. The crowded schedule and distances between venues left little discretionary time, but on Sunday, April 19, Johnny Cash unexpectedly broke away and rebooked his afternoon flight from Sydney to Brisbane to have a few extra hours in Sydney. The star's nonappearance when his tour group touched down in Brisbane disappointed a waiting airport crowd that included a bevy of journalists who had come to meet the celebrated singer. His whereabouts unknown, Cash managed to spend the balmy afternoon blending anonymously into a crowd of some sixty thousand at Sydney's Showground, where Graham's Southern Cross Crusade was in full swing. Cash knew of Graham but had never seen him, and the opportunity to blend in privately seemed too good to miss. When Graham's afternoon service ended, Cash caught the late flight to Brisbane, where a lone reporter camped out at the airport discovered the reason for Cash's delay. Cash obliged him with a terse comment on Graham (he was "very impressed," he said) and turned to the business at hand. As fate would have it, the next evening Cash's audience overflowed Brisbane's Milton Tennis Stadium, the same venue that exactly two weeks later would be hard pressed to accommodate the launch of Graham's Brisbane crusade.

Eleven years later, in 1970, Cash strode confidently into his second Graham crusade. This time he entered the stadium alongside Graham, cameras flashing all around, following the evangelist to a first-row center seat on the platform. The site was the University of Tennessee's Neyland Stadium in Knoxville, where sixty-two thousand people had assembled for day three of Graham's East Tennessee Crusade. Waters and Shea were the announced musicians alongside the mass choir, and Cash's appearance was a surprise treat and—as it turned out—a crusade turning point. Billy Graham himself presented Cash and his entourage (the Tennessee Three, the Carter Family Singers, Carl Perkins, and the Statler Brothers, all familiar regulars on the popular new *Johnny Cash Show* that aired weekly on ABC TV from the Grand Ole Opry's Ryman Auditorium) to the Sunday afternoon crowd. Graham seemed uncharacteristically at a loss for words, quipping that it was easier to introduce the president of the United States than to find words to describe Johnny Cash. Quoting a recent conversation with Bob Hope, Graham simply said that at that moment, Cash stood alone at the pinnacle of the American music world.

When Cash took the microphone, he explained that a few months before, Graham had called to ask if he could visit the Cash home. He flew from Asheville, North Carolina, to Hendersonville, Tennessee, and stayed overnight with John and June Cash. Cash recalled in his autobiography that he hoped for an invitation to sing at a crusade, but Graham did not broach the subject. They spent hours talking, and a friendship was born. Before Graham left, Cash volunteered to sing at a crusade whenever Graham wanted him. Graham called in the offer and invited him to Knoxville. After participating in a few more crusades, John and June Cash decided to prioritize crusade appearances in their schedules.

There is another rendering of this story that suggests that Graham and Cash sat down to dinner specifically to discuss Johnny and June Carter Cash's participation in crusades. That version credits Franklin Graham (then seventeen) with suggesting that his father contact Cash in order to tap into the vast audience the couple would certainly attract. By this account, the Graham organization worked through a mutual acquaintance to solicit an invitation to the Cash estate in Hendersonville. However the meeting came about, it resulted in a close and lifelong friendship between the couples. They frequently vacationed together at the Cash estate in Jamaica and elsewhere, enjoyed extended visits in each other's homes, and worked together, according to Cash, on at least thirty occasions in crusades, on movie sets, and in recording studios.

At his first Graham crusade, Cash and his group sang four numbers. For the first time at a crusade, organ and piano sat silent as Cash and his backup team strummed and sang. Cash briefly urged the audience to shun drugs but turned down an opportunity to give his own testimony, saying he would rather hear Graham. Cash was given the honor of singing directly before the sermon, a place on the program ordinarily reserved for a crowd-calming solo by Shea. Now thunderous applause filled the stadium as the final notes of a rousing "The Old Account Was Settled Long Ago" faded. Cash was a star in his own right, a man to whom audiences responded in predictable ways. Graham's preference for no applause had already yielded frequently over the years to Waters's crowd appeal. Johnny Cash was a still larger presence, and the applause could not be stopped. Barrows stepped forward, going off program to lead the crowd in the familiar words of "Trust and Obey." The crowd quieted, and Graham took the podium.

The Cash who faced the crowd that Sunday afternoon was no stranger to Graham's gospel. The son of hardworking Arkansas farmers, Cash was

the fourth of seven children of Ray and Carrie Cash. He came of age surrounded by hymns and folk and field songs. The family farmed twenty
acres in Dyess Colony, a New Deal–sponsored community in northeastern
Arkansas. With his siblings, he worked long hours in the cotton fields. The
family frequently attended special services at the nearby Church of God,
but their regular church home was the First Baptist Church of Dyess. There
Johnny Cash—his mother at the piano—sang his first solo, "The Unclouded
Day," an anticipation of heaven penned by the nineteenth-century circuit-
riding Brethren pastor Josiah Alwood. And there, soon after his twelfth
birthday in 1944, Cash attended every night of a two-week revival. One
fateful night as the congregation sang "Just as I Am," he walked forward,
shook the preacher's hand, and knelt with other penitents. It was, as he
recalled in *Man in Black*, the "direction choosing time" in his life, and Cash
chose Christ. As he matured, songs nurtured his spiritual life: he used them
to talk to God. They were, he said, "his telephone to heaven, and [he] tied
up the line quite a bit."

After high school, Cash enlisted in the air force. While in basic training in San Antonio, he fell in love with Vivian Liberto, a seventeen-year-
old Catholic girl of half-Sicilian ancestry with a mixed-race great-great-
grandmother in her maternal family tree. In 1954, a few weeks after his
three-year deployment ended, the couple married in a Catholic church in
San Antonio. In the army, Cash had gradually stopped practicing his faith,
but he could not get away from the tug of the gospel woven through the
lyrics of the songs that shaped him. He eventually gained an audience in
Nashville with Sam Phillips at Sun Records, the label that launched Elvis
Presley in 1954. At Sun, Cash produced a succession of charting singles.
Occasionally he sat around a piano there to sing gospel hymns with peers
who, like him, shared a complex relationship with the faith of their childhood, including one famous instance captured by photographers—the
"Million Dollar Quartet"—Cash with Elvis Presley, Carl Perkins, and Jerry
Lee Lewis. In 1956, he made his debut at the Grand Ole Opry. His signature
song, "I Walk the Line," sold over two million copies and remained on the
Billboard charts for forty-three weeks. Cash wrote those lyrics for his wife,
who was unhappy with the demands Cash's burgeoning music career made
on family life, but he later told journalist Robert Hilburn that the song was
in reality his first "gospel hit." He maintained a grueling tour schedule,

filling between two hundred and three hundred engagements annually. In late 1957, Cash moved to Columbia Records.

As he catapulted to fame, Cash's personal life spiraled out of control. His obsession with music undermined his marriage. His demanding schedule drove him to rely on amphetamines and barbiturates, and his growing infatuation with the married June Carter led Vivian Cash to file for divorce in 1966. She was awarded primary custody of the couple's four daughters.

For years, Cash's schedule had intersected professionally with that of the Carter Family, the legendary first family of country music. He first met June Carter backstage at the Grand Ole Opry. Each was married to another, but the pull of attraction was strong from the start. In 1962, Carter joined Cash's tour. June Carter's mother, Maybelle, was one of the original Carter Family Singers, and, with their daughter, and her husband, Ezra—a man well versed in Scripture—the Carters came alongside Cash at some of his lowest moments. In the meantime, June Carter did her best to persuade Cash to give up drugs and alcohol. In October 1967, Cash reached a low point. Addiction forced him to cancel shows. Drugs dried out his throat. Shamed by several arrests, plagued by guilt, unable to eat or sleep, Cash believed he had wandered too far from God to return. One day he drove to a cave along the Tennessee River and began crawling, intending to disappear forever in the labyrinth of caverns that ran under the Tennessee mountains.

In his autobiography, Cash described what happened as he agonized over his failures: first a sensation of "peace, clarity, and sobriety," followed by a conviction that he was not in charge of his destiny. Rather, God was. God had never left him: he had abandoned God. With difficulty, Cash crawled from the cave, returned to his vehicle, and found his mother and June Carter waiting. Carter had flown in from California overcome by the sense that Cash was in trouble. Carrie Cash had prayed regularly for her son and seldom lost an opportunity to remind him that she knew God had work for him to do. Now she heard him admit that he was ready to renew his relationship with God and to do whatever it took to clean up his life.

A month later Cash resumed his appearances. His divorce was finalized, as was Carter's, and in 1968 they married. The two began attending Nashville's Evangel Temple, an independent congregation pastored by Jimmie Snow, son of country music legend Hank Snow. There he heard an as-yet-undiscovered Larry Gatlin sing "Help Me," and Cash knew he had come home:

> I never thought I needed help before, . . .
> Now I know I just can't take it any more.
> With a humble heart, on bended knee,
> I'm beggin' You, please, help me.

Later in 1968 Cash performed a live concert at California's Folsom Prison, where he rerecorded his 1955 hit "Folsom Prison Blues." The song soared to number one on the country music charts. He returned as well to New York's Carnegie Hall, the site of one of his most embarrassing failures. In 1962, Carnegie Hall had featured an evening of country music, and critics expected much of the wildly popular Cash. Instead, high on drugs, Cash could not complete his program. The Carter Family stepped up, but a critic blasted his hoarse voice and incohesive program. "Another hearing is needed before his name can be mentioned among the other reputable country stars who were there," the *New York Times* critic concluded. In 1968, Cash made his comeback. The Carter Family, Carl Perkins, and the Tennessee Three shared the billing, but this time music critic Robert Shelton declared the evening "mostly a triumph for Johnny Cash, a special talent, happily back in the driver's seat." Cash said simply, "Sobriety suits me."

A long 1969 article in the *New York Times Magazine* by Arkansas journalist Thomas Dearborn celebrated the newly sober Johnny Cash as "the sizzling apogee of the country music market." Cash stood alone at the top. He sold more records and drew larger crowds than anyone else. Dearborn described Cash's voice as "the hottest seller in the spectrum." The "cotton-field hand turned millionaire singer and returnee from the depths of drug-use dissolution" was riding a national wave of interest in country music that he had helped to start.

In 1970, John and June Carter Cash accepted an invitation to sing at the Nixon White House. Their usual entourage accompanied them, but Johnny Cash was the unchallenged star of the hourlong concert before 225 guests. Cash's appearance at Graham's Knoxville crusade followed hard on his White House visit. On the *Johnny Cash Show*, he declared himself a Christian and often interspersed songs of faith among his musical selections.

Despite his strong comeback, Cash continued to struggle with addiction in the years that followed. Painkillers taken after a fall and surgery contributed to a new bout of dependency. A few days before Christmas in 1983, Cash sought treatment at the Betty Ford Center. He emerged after forty-three days with a keener sense of his need to rely daily on God's power to overcome his weakness. In his song "I Came to Believe," he told of how when he tried to handle his problems on his own, he failed and felt twice as alone. But when he cried to the Lord for a better way,

> I came to believe in a power much higher than I
> I came to believe that I needed help to get by
> In childlike faith I gave in and gave him a try
> Then I came to believe in a power much higher than I.

Graham stood by Cash through the difficult times, and Cash was brutally honest with crusade audiences about his struggles. His vulnerability lent authenticity to Graham's message of redemption. The platform regulars had never strayed far from their parents' God, but Cash knew firsthand the depths of helplessness. Cash was a vivid object lesson of what the Salvation Army described as "a trophy of grace."

Cash once discussed with Graham the possibility of exchanging his music career for the work of an evangelist. The two spent hours discussing the pros and cons before Graham advised Cash rather to combine faith and career. Cash followed that advice in part with appearances at Graham crusades, movies, and special events, and in part by integrating faith into his performances. The Graham team believed that crusade crowds were larger when Cash participated, and Cash increased Graham's audience by allotting him time on the *Johnny Cash Show*. Their relationship was common knowledge and was featured in 1971 in the first track on Cash's *Billboard* number-one country album, *Man in Black*. The two performed "Preacher Said-Jesus Said" on the *Johnny Cash Show*, with Johnny singing verses in which he questions what is true, complains about the greed in a world full of need, and asks how he can find the road to heaven, and Graham appearing obscured in shadow against a cross and reciting the words of Jesus from Scripture. Here's a taste:

Cash: "Oh you'd better tell us preacher before it's too late
         And then the preacher said of heaven Jesus said."

Graham: "Jesus said, 'Seek first the kingdom of God and
              his righteousness
         And all these things shall be added unto you.'"

Throughout their remaining careers and lives, Waters, Rogers and Evans, Cash and Carter remained closely identified with Billy Graham crusades. Other distinguished artists appeared less regularly, but they simi-
larly brought both their listening publics and their prestige to Graham's
platform. Among the more frequent, and broadly influential, crusade
performers and contributors were multiplatinum songwriters and singers
William James (Bill) and Gloria Gaither. Indiana-based gospel music singers, composers, and entrepreneurs, the Gaithers were enormously influential in revitalizing American congregational singing, nurturing young
talent, and identifying a lucrative market for the old standards of southern
gospel music.

The Gaithers began modestly in 1956 with the Bill Gaither Trio (the first
members were Bill and his siblings); they led the music in a small church
near their home in Alexandria, Indiana. Bill and Gloria met while teaching
high school there and wed in 1962. By 1967 their growing musical careers
enabled them to relinquish their high school jobs to devote themselves
full time to music. The couple produced songs, subjected them to a sifting
process by trying them out with the local church choir and the trio, and they
worked tirelessly to forge the links that would assure their future success.
A connection to the Graham organization was an obvious route to be ex-
plored. A song featured as a solo or choir number in a crusade and aired on
radio and television was guaranteed to reach a far larger audience than any
other option at their disposal. The problem for any musical start-up trying
to connect with the BGEA was getting a foot in the door.

By the 1960s, crusade music was as systematized as every other part of
each Graham endeavor. Planning began years in advance and musical strategy and selections moved through a series of committees. In the process,
Barrows and Shea regularly turned down new music sent their way by enter-

prising artists and composers. Some of the letters were by turns heart wrenching and head slapping. People presented melodies and proposed settings for poems they had been "given" by the Holy Spirit; inexperienced would-be singers offered their talents with the confidence that God would transform them into first-class artists if only Barrows heeded God's will and made room for them. A surprising number of people regularly implied that Graham's musicians were standing in the way of their chance to make a mark.

Barrows and Shea had no dilemma in maintaining tight standards for crusade material and performance, but by the early 1960s, the occasional new artist who merited their attention sometimes found it difficult to reach them. Bill Gaither was one of those who could not get past the gatekeepers and secretaries who opened the mail at BGEA headquarters. Unknown but determined, he figured out a way to make an end run around the gears of the BGEA machinery. At the end of March 1963, he addressed a letter to Shea at the Los Angeles office of one of Shea's music publishers and included a packet of handwritten mimeographed songs for his consideration: "I know this is taking 'a shot in the dark,' but I hope this letter gets past the front office and secretaries. Under a separate cover I have sent you a few songs that I have written. Would you PLEASE look at them and see if they would be of value to you?"

The materials eventually did reach Shea, but nothing came of the request. Then, in 1964, the Bill Gaither Trio recorded their breakthrough song "He Touched Me." An instant success with gospel groups, religious radio stations, and congregations across North America, by 1972 Elvis Presley was using it as the title track on a Grammy-winning inspirational album. Naturally, the song came to Barrows's attention, and he contacted Gaither for permission to use it. That phone conversation, augmented by the growing popularity of other Gaither compositions, began a long-term relationship. The couple first performed live at a crusade at the Toronto Skydome in 1978. They had played some large arenas, but, Gaither recalled in *Billy Graham and Me*, "we hadn't performed at that level yet." Dignitaries crowded the platform, the choir numbered in the thousands, and some sixty thousand people jammed every open space. Gaither remembered returning—usually with the Gaither Vocal Band—to crusade platforms more than twenty times. He sang at the "final" crusade in New York in 2005, the three-day extravaganza that began the original team's long farewell. From the 1980s forward, when neither Gaither was physically present, chances were good that sometime during every crusade one or another of their songs found a place as a solo, a congregational song, or a choral number.

The Gaithers' entrepreneurial instincts led them in multiple directions over the years. In 1976, they released what became a stunningly successful hymnal, *Hymns for the Family of God*. Edited by the well-respected church musician Fred Bock, the collection featured familiar hymns and gospel songs but made room as well for the popular songs of people like Ralph Carmichael ("Reach Out to Jesus"), Andraé Crouch ("The Blood Will Never Lose Its Power"), Kurt Kaiser ("Pass It On"), Stuart Hamblen ("It Is No Secret," "Until Then"), Larry Norman ("I Wish We'd All Been Ready"), and a long list of contributions from the Gaithers, including "He Touched Me," "The King Is Coming," "The Longer I Serve Him," "Because He Lives," "Family of God," and "Get All Excited." The Gaithers' inspirational music was wildly popular, suited to congregational use, and adaptable to various styles of accompaniment. *Hymns for the Family of God* carried forward the long tradition of introducing the new songs people wanted (or those hymnal editors wanted to test in the marketplace) in independently published hymnals. The process of winnowing was ongoing. Once people had clamored for the inclusion of Fanny Crosby. Now she and other gospel songwriters gave way to promoters of a different sound. With a long view, *Hymns for the Family of God* seemed more of an innovation than it was: it bore witness yet again to the dynamic nature of Christian song. Turning popular favorites people knew from concerts, movie soundtracks, radio, and recording artists into congregational hymnody presented church musicians with options for the sanctuary that had potential to renew congregational singing. It also hinted at larger changes ahead.

Over the decades, the music world has showered recognition on the Gaithers, beginning in 1969 when Gloria Gaither won the Dove Award for Songwriter of the Year. She won the award seven times in the next eight years—perhaps fittingly, as Bill Gaither is credited with originating the idea of the Dove Award at a 1968 meeting of the Gospel Music Association (GMA) Board. The GMA (established 1964) bestows the annual awards in recognition of excellence in Christian and gospel music, and over the decades, Dove Awards have celebrated an ever-richer stylistic diversity. At the fiftieth Dove Awards ceremony in 2019, the Gaither Vocal Band garnered yet another nomination. The Bill Gaither Trio won its first Grammy in 1977 for "Let's Just Praise the Lord." The Gospel Music Hall of Fame inducted Bill Gaither in 1983 and Gloria Gaither in 1997. In 2000, the American Society of Authors, Composers, and Publishers recognized the Gaithers with its Christian Songwriter of the Century award. Over the years, several Christian institutions honored Gloria Gaither's accomplishments as an author with honorary doctorates.

The Gaithers not only supplied new hymns, performed and recorded them, and took leadership in the mushrooming activities of the GMA, they also created the Gaither Music Company to coordinate the many aspects of their blossoming enterprises—record and television production, recording (the Gaither Studio), marketing, concert booking, copyright oversight. Their endeavors offered opportunities to emerging artists, and many young contemporary Christian performers broke into the industry by touring with the Gaithers before embarking on independent careers. In this indirect way, they exerted influence on the musical artists featured at later Graham crusades.

In 1991, Bill Gaither conceived the idea of sponsoring *Homecoming* (concerts, videos, and recordings), a concept that exploded well beyond his own very modest expectations. Gaither often repeated the standard story of *Homecoming*'s beginning. In 1991, bookings for the Gaither Vocal Band (which succeeded the Bill Gaither Trio in 1981) were down, a new generation of artists and a new sound in Christian music dominated the airwaves, and the Gaithers decided they were ready to slow down, if not quite retire. Bill wanted to record one more album with the Gaither Vocal Band under the title *Homecoming*, and he seized on the idea of convening as many of the legends of southern gospel music as he could convince to join the Gaither Vocal Band for one number—"Where Could I Go but to the Lord?" Gaither had come of age listening to southern gospel albums. These folks had been his childhood musical heroes, though several had fallen on hard times as musical tastes changed.

A good representation of those white gospel singers responded and met Gaither at a Nashville recording studio. When the studio session concluded, the group simply could not stop singing the old standards. They sang from memory with no program. The tape kept rolling. Gaither marketed the informal video recording, and the overwhelmingly positive response led to annual professionally produced events, part sing-along, part concert, and replete with reminiscences from the southern gospel greats whose careers now took on new energy. The old-timers sat on stage in the first row, while younger artists gathered behind them, and enormous live audiences thrilled to the sounds. *Homecoming* videos—often themed or recorded in special locations—occasionally reached number one on *Billboard*'s music video chart; several garnered Dove Awards; all reaped enormous financial profit. Gaither's career took on new life. The Gaither Vocal Band continued, and *Homecomings* proved an elastic idea that could accommodate family fests, songwriting workshops, and Alaska cruises.

The idea of homecoming resonated in a mobile society. To be sure, Gaither *Homecomings* were filled with nostalgia, but they were more than a trip down memory lane. In a real sense, the songs invited people "home" by evoking memories of church, childhood, and family. The songs were far more than lyrics and tunes. The act of singing summoned singers back to settings replete with people, places, religious experiences, and the values that had shaped them. For many, the songs said something fundamental about their identity. But the Gaithers were savvy businesspeople. They knew well that musical styles and tastes were changing. They needed to keep *Homecoming* relevant, and so in time they carefully blended newer musical impulses while preserving the signature sound.

Several *Homecoming* celebrations featured the music of the Graham crusades, along with Barrows and Shea as special guests. Ruth Graham joined the event at the Cove in Asheville in 2001. In 2011, a tent on the grounds of the Billy Graham Library in Charlotte accommodated the crowd for a concert by gospel music legends alongside Barrows and Shea. Shea, then 102 years old, accepted a commemorative copy of *Billboard* magazine in which a Gaither *Homecoming* special featuring Shea had charted at number three in the music video category.

Graham crusades relied on an array of musical idioms and many voices to sing the "one song" that every crusade featured. For each service, Barrows recruited every platform guest to share the no-nonsense evangelistic imperative that drove Graham, Barrows, Shea, and their accompanists. All of this was managed, though, without displacing Barrows and Shea, who, when all was said and done, still carried the brand at every crusade.

From the 1970s forward, though, youth movements increasingly transformed society and broadly challenged the musical idioms traditionally featured in Christian song. Crusade music followed a middle path, featuring "the best" gospel songs interspersed among traditional hymns, but pressure to expand the repertoire came from several sources, internal and external. The situation was complicated by the aging of the platform team. In 1969, Shea celebrated his sixtieth birthday, Graham his fifty-first. They were middle-aged men, and some thought they had long left behind the appeal to youth that marked their earlier years as a team. The antiestablishment inclinations of the youth culture—to say nothing of youthful anti-Vietnam War demonstrators, civil rights activists, and feminists—challenged the church as well as the culture and forced hard thinking about relevance. The main issue was simple: the "one thing" Graham's crusades had always emphasized remained the "one thing" in every age. There was no need to alter the message. But might the contemporary music idiom that captured the youth culture's mood be a suitable tool to bring yet another generation to consider Graham's message? Should the Graham team translate the message—in particular settings, at least—into a new musical idiom?

TRANSLATION

What will people think when they hear that I'm a Jesus freak?
What will people do when they find that it's true?
I don't really care if they label me a Jesus freak
There ain't no disguising the truth.

—dc Talk, "Jesus Freak," 1995

At the end of March 1999, the GMA Hall of Fame announced its newest class of inductees. By custom, the association recognized influential artists and songwriters with at least twenty-five years in gospel music. The class of 1999 included veterans from a wide spectrum of gospel genres: the broadly popular Midwestern-based Bill Gaither Trio; the innovative black gospel group the Mighty Clouds of Joy; Nashville's own a cappella jubilee gospel singers, the Fairfield Four; the Second Chapter of Acts, a sibling trio that pioneered Jesus Music in the 1970s; southern gospel harmony groups the Cathedrals—and their influential bass singer George Younce—and the Florida Boys. And Billy Graham. With this honor, Graham joined a list of GMA-recognized sacred music luminaries that reached back before the emergence of a "gospel music industry," including such figures as eighteenth-century Methodist hymnist Charles Wesley (1995), "Amazing Grace" author John Newton (1982), and prolific nineteenth-century gospel stalwarts like Fanny Crosby (1975), P. P. Bliss (1989), and Ira D. Sankey (1980).

Graham hardly fit even the largest parameters of the GMA profile, and the honor surprised no one more than himself. His musical colleague George Beverly Shea had been inducted alongside Mahalia Jackson back in 1978, and Cliff Barrows had been the lone inductee in 1988. Frequent crusade artists like Ethel Waters and Stuart Hamblen were members of long standing. But Graham himself? Notified of the honor, he asked Shea, "Don't those people know I can't even sing a note?" The evangelist's lack of musical ability was an open secret. Years earlier Barrows had informed Graham that he would surely be unemployed in heaven since evangelistic preaching would not be needed, while he and Shea would be busier than ever with the heavenly choir.

The inductions took place during the third week of April 1999 in a hotel ballroom in downtown Nashville. Graham was the first nonmusician so honored, and GMA leaders deftly explained that they were recognizing Graham for his musical *influence* rather than his musical *skills*. "The Graham stage has opened its doors when some churches would not because Christian pop was too contemporary," the GMA commended. "They were smart enough to realize that this popular music was the vernacular the people were speaking." The inductees of the GMA Hall of Fame class of 1999 represented a blend of traditional and innovative music that accented generational differences in taste, and Graham's crusade platforms and media events had offered artists unprecedented access to new, mass audiences for five decades. "It is fitting to pay homage to what he has given our artists," remarked GMA president Frank Breeden.

Shea, then ninety years old, accepted the award on Graham's behalf, and gold record–winning Contemporary Christian Music (CCM) star Michael W. Smith, a frequent crusade guest, performed in Graham's honor. In prepared remarks, Shea noted Graham's long-standing recognition of the role of music in reaching people with the gospel message by softening listeners' hearts and opening their minds. In fact, for several years music had become an increasingly urgent point of discussion in Graham's circle.

Already in the 1980s journalists speculated about which crusade would be the aging trio's last. In the face of generational turnover, changing media, youth activism, and social upheaval, many wondered if three elderly men could continue to command the mass appeal they had enjoyed for decades.

They had, after all, begun in a movement known as Youth for Christ, but, as Shea quipped, they had become "old men for Christ." The three cared deeply about the next generation. Their longevity meant that they had, in fact, cared actively for several "next generations," and by most accounts, they had made a difference. For several decades, wherever the team went, under-twenty-fives composed the largest group of crusade respondents. But as the 1980s progressed, the percentage of youthful inquirers slowly declined, and some within the organization worried that the "good old days" had ended. Would modern youth throng to hear a seventy-five-year-old evangelist or thrill to the solos of an eighty-four-year-old gospel-singing legend?

Discussions about attendance and demographics often circled back to music. Two separate issues surfaced: first, crusade music in general; second, music for the youth nights that were part of every crusade. As fathers, grandfathers, and great-grandfathers familiar with the pressures on modern youth, the platform trio still felt "called" to the work that consumed them. Could they adapt successfully to the expectations of yet another generation? Media and music had been important components of a constantly evolving youth culture in the previous decades and opened an ever-widening gap with the BGEA's traditional musical approach.

Barrows had responsibility for crusade music, but his relationship with Shea meant that Shea's opinion mattered, too, and forty years of international crusades had shown all three members of the team that music always touched a nerve—no matter what they did, critics were ever ready to pounce. Their decades of experience had also taught them that their choices on sensitive matters had the potential to influence congregational practice. Barrows's musical direction reflected their overall, hard-won consensus: different musical styles could be appropriate in different settings. The music he selected for World Wide Pictures might never feature on a crusade platform, but it suited its purpose. During crusade preparations, Barrows responded to the wishes of one segment of their churchgoing constituency by expressing his personal distaste for using what he called "beat music" in the crusades proper or on the *Hour of Decision*. On this same subject, Shea had been atypically forthright from the 1950s, declaring his view that neither rock 'n' roll nor "Christian rock" had a place in Christian contexts. Graham's syndicated "My Answer" columns frequently addressed writers' concerns about the role of music and musical styles. How should adults react when a pastor substituted contemporary music for traditional hymns? If the preaching was biblical, did musical style even matter? The columns routinely counseled patience, communication, and prayer in the quest to save young souls.

Complicating the picture, the platform trio knew well the varied musical tastes of their own offspring. Like other parents, they remembered their own upbringings and worried about what music their children and grandchildren favored. Barrows regularly lectured on music and evangelism in the Schools of Evangelism run by the BGEA, and he admitted that his parents (who lived into the 1970s) considered rock 'n' roll "the devil's music" and would certainly have forbidden him to listen to it. Late in life, Barrows recalled his son's involvement in a traveling contemporary music evangelistic outreach that bore remarkable results. And so, he navigated the considerable pressures of his responsibilities with one eye to the goal of communicating a message and the other to an increasingly contentious discussion about Christian music.

Barrows was no stranger to sharp criticisms about crusade music. People often complained that crusade music was either outdated or too modern; others grumbled that the team allotted insufficient time for music, while still others opined that there was too much singing. One overarching change over the years had been a sharp curtailment of the time allotted for music from the choir, audience, and Shea to accommodate broadcast schedules and make room for guest artists. Whereas in 1957 at Madison Square Garden Barrows had ample time for a fifteen-minute hymn sing, by the time the team returned to the Garden in 1969, time constraints permitted just one congregational song and one Shea solo. Pressures about time allotments and—increasingly—musical genre continued to grow, and by the late 1980s a strong youth-driven preference for more contemporary styles pushed the aging trio to change.

Evidence of major shifts in musical preference among conservative American Protestants first began to appear in the mid-to-late 1960s, as the charismatic renewal and then the Jesus People Movement came of age alongside the Graham crusades. Their praise and worship choruses and blends of folk, pop, and rock sounds reshaped the evangelical musical landscape with what eventually came to be known as CCM. A growing list of performers and a cluster of new record labels catered to the tastes of younger audiences to influence Christian culture, as the line between worship, performance, and entertainment blurred.

During the 1960s, Graham had spoken at universities, mingled with protesters, and occasionally even wandered incognito into a rock festival. During this period, youth, reflecting both the size of the baby boom generation and the turmoil in American culture, constituted the majority of crusade respondents. In the bigger picture, Graham was deeply concerned by the evident dissatisfaction and rebelliousness of many young people, evidenced in the ubiquity of antiwar protests, the rise of the drug culture, and the increasingly permissive lifestyles ushered in with the burgeoning sexual revolution. This reinforced his calling as an evangelist and amplified his optimism about a youth revival he believed had begun with the Jesus People Movement. The revival was admittedly countercultural, sometimes faddish, often superficial, yet Graham found hope in its biblicism, discipleship, and emphasis on evangelism.

Graham knew firsthand the tensions in the contemporary youth culture. In the '60s and '70s he was dealing with the rebelliousness of his own sons. The deep conviction that youth represented the best hope of the nation drove a determination to understand the cultural idioms that conveyed their convictions and expressed their perceptions, including their contentious attachment to rock music.

During Graham's New York crusade in June 1969, the team first tried a new approach to youth evangelism. Each evening from nine until midnight, the crusade sponsored a coffeehouse in the seventh-floor ballroom of the Manhattan Center, a popular New York performance venue just a block from the crusade at the city's new Madison Square Garden (opened in 1968). In the '50s and '60s, coffeehouses had become popular venues for food, beverages, games, music, and conversation, oases for people exploring the youth counterculture that were viewed by many community leaders as "dissolute hangouts." In the late '60s, Christian outreaches turned to coffeehouses as a ministry opportunity, and the Graham crusade opted into the model. Admission was by a fifty-cent ticket available to high school and college-aged youth through church youth groups and at Madison Square Garden, and the 850 seats sold out every night, as did overflow on a lower level. The crusade provided Pepsi products, Fritos, and pretzels and gave the ballroom a club feel with flashing multicolored iridescent lights that served as a backdrop for performers. As people gathered, musicians—

including crusade pianist Tedd Smith—offered a mix of blues, jazz, and folk. After forty-five minutes, John Guest and the Exxkursions took the stage. Converted under Graham's preaching in Britain, Guest migrated to the United States in 1964 and eventually linked up with a Chicago-based blues-rock group called the Exxkursions that toured college campuses under the auspices of InterVarsity Christian Fellowship. At the crusade coffeehouse, the Exxkursions offered several numbers, among which were a few "message songs" that provided an easy segue to a Christian witness with a slide-show background. Up next would either be the Kinsfolk, an Australian folk group, or the Sons of Thunder, a newly formed Christian rock band with a recently released record titled "'Til the Whole World Knows." Table conversation guided by a counselor filled a brief intermission. After a third music segment, a brief gospel message and invitation concluded the evening.

Detailed follow-up assessments by pianist Smith and frequent crusade organist Donald Hustad concluded that addressing youth in their own musical idiom had merit. Smith noted that 99 percent were obviously "turned on" by the music and related to the performers. They listened willingly to the testimonies of musicians they admired. Smith professed that his involvement in the coffeehouse changed his life and ministry. All this contrasted with the comments he overheard about the crusade itself from the young people: "boring," "draggy music," "too much talking," "constant religion," "too many Bible-toting people shoving their way to the best seats."

In a continued response to the growing turmoil among youth and the role of rock music therein, Graham began to try and understand the phenomenon. At one point Billy and Ruth bought several rock albums and listened to them to glean insights into the social upheaval of the era. The Grahams knew that incorporating such music—even in its Christian guise—into crusade youth nights would inevitably raise an outcry, but Ruth joined a handful of staff in urging Graham to try a new approach. Christian rock would attract a different audience, they argued, and, as Ruth pointed out, it promised Billy a "larger pond" in which to fish for souls. The music was not "their" music, but it could become a vehicle for the translation of Graham's message into the idiom of the next generation. Thousands of young people were outside of the ordinary reach of the church. The Grahams weighed the options of inviting them in by employing a variation on the translation of their message.

In December 1969 Graham dropped into the Miami Rock Festival to better understand the younger generation and the rock festival scene and was actually invited to preach. With the recent Woodstock Festival still a vivid memory and a slew of other multiday rock festivals having been held across the country, the Miami festival organizers drew significant opposition from the community surrounding the concert venue, International Speedway in Hollywood. Worries about drugs, alcohol, promiscuity, and the general antiestablishment fervor associated with such festivals had locals up in arms about a program that featured some of the artists from Woodstock and attracted thousands of revelers to three days of performances by the likes of the Grateful Dead, Vanilla Fudge, Canned Heat, Santana, and the Paul Butterfield Blues Band. In an effort to reassure the community, festival organizers extended an invitation to Graham to speak before the music began on Sunday, December 28. The evangelist promptly accepted.

Graham spent a few hours on Saturday evening mingling with the festival crowds to get a feel for who they were. Canned Heat and Vanilla Fudge performed that night, and the music continued nonstop until 4 a.m. When Graham returned for his 11 a.m. Sunday morning engagement, he addressed a small crowd about the sentiments he had heard in their music, their rejection of materialism, and their longing for spiritual reality. He urged them to "get high without hang-ups and hangovers through Jesus." They were hardly his typical audience, but he seemed unfazed while some slept, others lolled about on scattered straw, and still others walked aimlessly, waiting for the music to begin. When Graham finished, perhaps a score of festivalgoers found their way to a small inquiry tent for prayer.

Graham's keen interest in youth culture continued. When *Life*, *Time*, *Newsweek*, *Look*, CBS, NBC, and other cultural observers heralded the "Jesus Revolution," Graham emerged as a warm—though not uncritical—supporter of a movement he believed contained the seeds of national revival. As grand marshal of the Tournament of Roses Parade on New Year's Day 1971, Graham raised a clenched fist with his index finger pointed upward in solidarity with hundreds of young people who lined the route displaying placards with Christian slogans and shouting, "One Way." Later in 1971 he published *The Jesus Generation*, a book that affirmed the youth revival and addressed "the alienated, uncommitted, rebellious majority of youth" who still needed Christ. By that time, Graham had already begun planning his role in a mammoth youth event scheduled for Dallas in June 1972. Campus Crusade for Christ founder Bill Bright had been inspired during a Graham Conference on Evangelism in Minneapolis to enlist young people in the task and organized Explo '72, an event that aimed to gather tens of thousands of high school and college young people for a week of evangelism training, hands-on experience, and massive evening rallies in the seventy-five-thousand-seat Cotton Bowl. Bright and his young staff had precise goals: bring the gospel to every American by 1976 and to the whole world by 1980. He named Graham honorary chairman, and Graham agreed to give six plenary addresses.

Some eighty thousand young people from all around the United States and Canada together with a few dozen internationals converged on Dallas in June 1972. They spent their mornings in one of sixty-five workshops on evangelism scattered in venues across the city. In the afternoons they went door to door and preached on Dallas streets. With his younger son in tow, Graham joined them in public witness, enthusing about the "thrilling and wonderful thing" God was doing among youth. Evening rallies jammed the Cotton Bowl, and Graham shared the limelight with the hottest names in the emerging genre of "Jesus Music" (later branded as CCM). He dubbed the event a Christian Woodstock. (Some preferred "Godstock.") While most young Americans shouted at concerts, protests, and drug festivals, said Graham, the Cotton Bowl echoed with "praise the Lord." At the last evening service, Graham led a candlelight consecration service that illuminated the stadium as thousands of young people declared their intent to evangelize their world. Eighty-five years earlier, the Student Volunteer Movement had enlisted thousands to evangelize the world "in this generation." These young people vowed to accomplish the task in eight years.

Explo '72 culminated in a massive nine-hour outdoor concert on an unfinished strip of downtown Dallas highway that featured the all-stars of an emerging Christian music: Johnny Cash, Love Song, Larry Norman, Randy Mathews, the Archers, Children of the Day, Willa Dorsey, the Armageddon Experience, and Andraé Crouch and the Disciples. Locals swelled the numbers until they approached 200,000. Vendors sold hats and soft drinks to crowds covering every inch of asphalt, grass, curb, vehicles, and roofs. As the event drew to a close, Graham addressed the throng, calling the day a "Christian happening" and one of the most thrilling experiences of his life.

Graham's unqualified endorsement of Explo '72 encouraged all aspects of the youth revival, including the Christian musicians experimenting with the new sounds of Christian rock. Graham freely admitted that he preferred other music, but he made a point of speaking positively about the contemporary youth revival as a work of God that reverenced the Bible, promoted the new birth, and prioritized evangelism.

Barrows and Shea were sensitive to change and eager to encourage the young musicians who took the crusade platform. All along, Barrows had attempted to mix up the youth-night sound by including a few more contemporary arrangements or popular stars among the regulars. He booked people he knew had a genuine testimony. During the heyday of *The Lawrence Welk Show* in the 1950s and '60s, Norma Zimmer, "The Champagne Lady," or her colleague, trumpeter Larry Zell, appeared at youth nights and on Graham specials. By the 1970s, youth rallies and crusade platforms featured British pop star Cliff Richard, country singer George Hamilton IV, and a succession of Jesus Music and CCM figures such as Evie (Evie Tornquist), Larnelle Harris, Twila Paris, Sandi Patti, Steven Curtis Chapman, and Michael W. Smith.

But as time passed, some people in the larger Graham organization urged that changing times required a more drastic break with the past. They proposed a youth night that would be half concert, half sermon, and invitation. The familiar trappings of Graham crusades—Barrows's genial greetings and firm control over the presermon program, prayers by visiting dignitaries, the mass choir, Bev Shea's solos, and "Just as I Am"—would be jettisoned. The idea was broached to Barrows in the latter part of the 1980s by crusade director Rick Marshall, with strong support from pianist Smith. The proposed change seemed so drastic that Barrows felt he needed to consult Graham. After mulling over the proposal, Graham agreed to "dress up the crusade" for youth. Yet, what seemed like a drastic change within the context of the forty-year crusade tradition was, in reality, much less novel in the larger scheme of Graham's long involvement with youth.

By the late 1980s, the rapidity of change and generational turnover had helped many church people to overcome early prejudices against CCM. Although it may not have been their own choice, the raucous sounds of pop no longer seemed so off-putting. Music shaped youth culture, and reaching youth appeared to demand flexibility in its idiom. Debates about music morphed into discussions about translation.

For forty years, Barrows and Shea had kept crusade music "conservative"—if it was not "highbrow" by mainline Protestant standards, it was at least "traditional" by evangelical standards. Outside observers tended to comment that Graham, Barrows, and Shea never changed despite massive cultural upheavals. Certainly, their accompanists abetted this perception, updating older harmonies but preserving live organ and piano for newer numbers, too. A closer look reveals a more complicated picture. Unlike Homer Rodeheaver, who cultivated a conspicuous taste for new songs (often with ties to his own publishing interests) at every revival, Graham's team relied on a handful of songs as crusade themes. Shea sang a particular type of solo, generally an old hymn or gospel song, but sometimes a number drawn from a solo, rather than a congregational, repertoire. Choir, congregation, and solos were all, and always, accompanied live by piano and organ. The frequency of crusades and the consistency of the music that framed their most important moments, however, tended to obscure two other trends that had been apparent from the outset.

First, Barrows and Shea *did* make extensive use of "contemporary" music, although admittedly what was "contemporary" in 1950 seemed tried-and-true by 1980. In significant ways, both men moved with the times but without relinquishing the classic sound that defined them. The music provided for congregational singing at crusades drew from contemporary songs by composers like John Peterson and Kurt Kaiser as well as traditional works, but Barrows maintained the aura of conservatism and comfort by keeping a church-friendly and familiar keyboard-based accompaniment.

Second, Barrows used crusade music to provide a mix of songs suited to place and occasion. Guest artists filled prominent roles from the first crusade in 1949, and they often brought songs and styles that resonated with various listening publics and genres within the world of popular music. Sometimes these guests enjoyed such popularity with crusade audiences that they continued to appear decades after their secular audience diminished. Take, for example, Ethel Waters, whose secular career climaxed before she became a frequent crusade soloist. Barrows often selected guest artists with attention to region and ethnicity: Native Americans might be called upon in Albuquerque or a Mexican or Filipino singer in Southern California. Abroad he took recommendations for guest artists from host committees. As the years rolled by, he frequently used experienced guest artists who sang CCM. Sometimes Barrows took a chance on an inexperienced singer who came well recommended (as he did with a relatively unknown nineteen-year-old Amy Grant in 1979). In every case, he made sure that platform participants had a sure and publicly recognized Christian witness.

Congregational singing remained anchored in a handful of old favorites even as it made way for new songs. At the outset, "current" meant Oswald J. Smith's "Then Jesus Came." In the 1960s, it included John W. Peterson's "Surely Goodness and Mercy." From the 1970s on, "current" embraced selections from a more contemporary Christian music repertoire that had begun transforming evangelical worship. A glance at crusade song sheets for congregational use from the 1980s finds "To God Be the Glory" side by side with "Give Thanks with a Grateful Heart" (Henry Smith, 1978) or "He Has Made Me Glad" (Leona von Brethorst, 1976). In each venue, Barrows attempted to find a common denominator to help people respond. At the outset, he and Shea knew most of the artists who joined them on crusade platforms, but decades on, Smith and Barrows began to consult with local youth leaders about which artists would draw a young crowd.

From the outset the Graham team had kept youth in focus, and youth around the globe had been responsive. Crusades built children's rallies and youth services into the schedule. In the early years, tens of thousands of children flocked to Saturday morning special events where Barrows ("Uncle Cliff") galvanized them with dramatic reenactments of biblical stories like "Naaman the Leper" (also available in comic-book format under Barrows's name), "Uncle Billy" made five-minute remarks, and "Uncle Bev" sang "Heavenly Sunshine." Children responded by the hundreds to the invitation to receive Christ. By the 1990s, Psalty the Singing Songbook with the Kids' Touring Company, along with Jungle Jam and the Friendship Company, had taken over the program (renamed "Kidz Gigs"), but Barrows still convened mass children's choirs (usually between two and four thousand strong) for the events.

The proposal for changes in the 1990s faced several hurdles. First was the music itself. As "Jesus Music" became "Contemporary Christian Music," there were new subgenres of youth-oriented music—heavy metal, grunge, rap, and hip-hop—that continued to fuel detractors who associated anything smacking of rock music with drugs, sex, and rebellion. A second hurdle was the long tradition of evangelistic crusades. For over forty years, Graham crusades had followed a pattern, and each component of every crusade fulfilled a purpose. Graham crusades resembled the crusades of earlier evangelists reaching back to the earliest days of American history. Turning a crusade service into a rock concert followed by a brief sermon eliminated or minimized the traditional roles of local clergy, congregational singing, the choir, the longtime soloist (Shea had a perfect attendance record at domestic crusades), the accompanists, and the platform director, whose vision for the whole service kept things moving toward the sermon and its climax in the invitation. These items were not merely components of a program. From the 1940s, Barrows expressed strong convictions about each. Would tampering with the usual flow of a service by removing elements long deemed essential have unanticipated negative implications? How might it ultimately influence the impact of crusades as a whole? Graham often expressed his preference for a Shea solo immediately preceding his sermon to quiet crowds and prepare his own heart for ministry. Could a rock band fill that role? With Graham's support, the team made plans to see. Neither Barrows nor Shea participated in the call for change. Both had reservations, but once a decision was made within the larger planning team, they presented a united front with Graham. As he had done in many different situations over the years, Barrows stepped up to help a new format succeed. The longtime platform trio agreed that a clear presentation of a biblical message mattered most, and Barrows made it his business to be sure that happened.

The new format for crusade youth nights debuted in Cleveland in June 1994. The crusade itself ran from Wednesday to Sunday, June 8 to 12, at the cavernous Cleveland Stadium, the site of Graham's 1972 Cleveland crusade, with Saturday the eleventh set aside for a morning children's rally and an evening youth concert. Ads promoted a free concert with the hottest Christian band at the time—dc Talk—along with successful crossover artist Michael W. Smith, and a featured testimony from Cleveland Cavaliers all-pro point guard Mark Price. The new format touched all aspects of crusade preparation. Planning for the concert included area church youth groups, who gathered at Cleveland Stadium ahead of the crusade for two evenings of Christian bands and motivational talks from nationally known youth speaker Ron Hutchcraft. Holding hands, they formed an enormous prayer chain and followed Graham's twenty-four-year-old grandson, Jonathan Lotz, in a prayer that the stadium would be "filled with the Holy Spirit." "This is not entertainment," Lotz reminded them, "but an effort to reach youths with the gospel." Advertising targeted the area's rock stations (they heavily promoted the concert) and local spots embedded within MTV programming. Ads promoted the event as "The First Concert to Benefit Its Own Audience." Print ads featured the music over the speakers: "dc Talk and Michael W. Smith with Mark Price and Billy Graham."

While crusade platforms typically measured 60 feet, a rock concert for a venue the size of Cleveland Stadium required a 100-foot stage, this one centered near the 50-yard-line of the football field. Trucks brought in the equipment for a huge light show, and crusade organizers rented three of the four Jumbotrons then available in the United States. Not surprisingly, the flow of the service had to be adjusted. Barrows would be nowhere in sight. He and Shea sat the event out in the press box. Before the service, though, Barrows reviewed with the musicians the lyrics of every song they planned to sing, arranged for their reading of Scripture, and made sure all participants knew their place in the flow of the proceedings. The plan included having dc Talk introduce Graham as a friend who had something to say to the crowd. Graham would be introduced as a grandfatherly figure, a wise older man with good advice, someone the band trusted and commended to their fans.

At the time, the interracial pop/rap/hip-hop/rock trio dc Talk enjoyed phenomenal popularity. Formed by Liberty University students Toby McKeehan ("Toby Mac"), Michael Tait, and Kevin Max Smith ("Kevin Max"), dc Talk had reinvented CCM by fusing elements of rap and a heavy, danceable beat with Christian lyrics. The band's 1992 album *Free at Last* catapulted them to fame with six chart singles, a Grammy for Best Rock Gospel Album, and double platinum sales (two million copies sold). For a record thirty-four weeks, it topped *Billboard* magazine's Christian charts. In 1991 and 1993, dc Talk had been the opening act for Grammy and Dove Award–winning Michael W. Smith, who had recently scored a certified gold record for the song "Place in This World" that had "crossed over" into the pop charts. While Smith's brand of upbeat pop and anthemic ballads was broadly mainstream, dc Talk's music was much closer to the cutting edge of the emerging rap and alternative rock norms of the '90s. Nonetheless, the group's lyrics, like most of Smith's, were emphatically Christian.

When the heavily promoted day arrived, the prospects of a free concert by the country's top Christian band and a celebrated solo artist drew sixty-five thousand young people to Cleveland Stadium, the largest crowd of the crusade. Opening the evening extravaganza was the Maranatha Praise Band—part of Calvary Chapel Costa Mesa's music label—with songs like "Let the Walls Fall Down," "I Will Celebrate," and Rick Founds's newly popular "Lord, I Lift Your Name on High." The crowd went wild when hometown basketball hero Mark Price appeared on the screens, and then began jumping, screaming, and swirling when dc Talk took the stage. Michael Tait's braided hair, along with the trio's ripped jeans and gyrating stage antics, a local paper reported, made the group seem "like clones of any other MTV act." Their part of the evening was noisy and energetic with beach ball–tossing and teenagers screaming and jumping. The singers leaped and climbed about the stage while performing such recent hits as "Luv Is a Verb" and a remake of the 1960s' hit "Jesus Is Just Alright" from their platinum-selling album, *Free at Last*. "There's a lot of people who say Jesus is all wrong," rapper Toby Mac belted into the microphone. "But I'm here to tell you JESUS. IS. STILL. ALL. RIGHT!" After six high-energy numbers, dc Talk yielded the stage to Michael W. Smith, who opened with a music video, "Secret Ambition," from his 1988 platinum album *I 2 (Eye)*, accompanied by a video on a giant screen behind the stage projecting New Testament scenes. He had the stadium on its feet with "Place in This World" and "the ever-so-popular tear-jerker, 'Friends.'" Smith, whose wife was a graduate of Graham's alma mater, Wheaton College, had participated in an earlier crusade as pianist for Amy Grant and was on his way to developing a personal friendship with the Grahams.

As darkness fell over Cleveland Stadium, a golf cart drove quietly across the field bringing Graham to center stage, and "a palpable change" came over the raucous crowd. The audience welcomed him with a rousing standing ovation, and he joked that he was "the anticlimax" of the party. His sermon was shorter than usual and billed as "a straight talk from a caring adult." It even commended the music—"You've heard the gospel through what they sang." Graham mentioned the recent suicide of rocker Kurt Cobain and segued into his message on John 3:16 with a reference to Arnold Schwarzenegger's mega-hit *Terminator 2: Judgment Day*. "They listened all the way," Graham told a press conference. "It was quiet enough to hear a pin drop." The Maranatha Singers provided musical support for Graham's invitation with a heartfelt rendering of "I Need You," as over 6,500 youths flocked to the stage in response. The number caught organizers off guard, and counselors were in short supply. Earlier that Saturday, in the morning, more than 3,000 children had responded to the gospel as told by Psalty the Singing Songbook, the Doughnut Man, and Charity Church Mouse from a stage decorated to resemble a Saturday morning children's television set. The evening event brought the total number of decisions for Saturday, June 11, to just shy of 10,000, while the day's attendance at both events approached 90,000.

Graham's Northeast Ohio Crusade had unquestionably found a responsive youthful audience. One concertgoer told the *Cleveland Plain Dealer*, "I love the music. I think this is what heaven is going to be like. I think heaven will be jammin' and kickin'." Journalists applauded Graham's "revamped gospel delivery" that tuned in to the sensibilities of a new generation, while religious leaders acknowledged the risk he took when many considered rock 'n' roll "an area of Christian compromise." Graham himself admitted: "Personally, I didn't understand a word of those songs [as they were being sung]. But I had all the lyrics written down, and they were straight Bible, great lyrics."

Although the crowds that jammed the lakefront stadium for the concert never saw him, Barrows was very much there, and he saw to it that all those lyrics Graham had been following were printed and distributed to each concertgoer. He had spent much of Saturday afternoon with the evening's performers, planning the service and praying with them for the event. Whether onstage or off, he took seriously his responsibility for assuring that the audience heard the gospel through every crusade presentation. Being the sponsor of a rock concert brought him an unexpected new chore, too. Left to themselves, singers ran, jumped, climbed, did handstands, and moved constantly and quickly about the stage and the props. The next week, Barrows took calls from crusade insurers, and at future concerts he curtailed musicians' more rambunctious moves.

Later that summer, Ruth and Billy Graham welcomed dc Talk for a cordial follow-up visit at their home in Montreat, North Carolina. A few months later, they met again at Graham's second youth concert, this time a Saturday evening at the Georgia Dome, in Atlanta, that ads promoted as "Jammin' at the Dome." The November 1994 crusade was Graham's third in Atlanta. The first in 1950 was at the Ponce de Leon Ballpark, home of the minor league Atlanta Crackers. The opening service there attracted 25,000, Graham's largest audience anywhere to that point. The first *Hour of Decision* broadcast was beamed from that crusade on November 5, 1950. Graham had returned to Atlanta in 1973, to Fulton County Stadium, for a weeklong crusade attended by Jimmy Carter, Andrew Young, and Coretta Scott King but loudly criticized by civil rights activists Ralph Abernathy and Hosea Williams, who objected to Graham's noninvolvement in their form of civil rights activism.

With that experience in mind, Graham made the five-day 1994 crusade at the 74,000-seat Georgia Dome absolutely contingent on the support of African American churches, enlisting several prominent pastors. Over 332,000 people attended the meetings, and the music program featured several noted black artists, including Andraé Crouch and his backup group. Crouch, who had sung for crusades since the 1970s, was joined by Marietta, Georgia's own Babbie Mason. Mason's blend of pop, soul, and praise and worship in her Christian chart-topping single "A World of Change" embodied the team's view of the crusade. She sang that because God did not see color, Christians could love one another.

> In God's eyes there is no color, . . .
> Because we have a faith in common,
> There's hope for each tomorrow,
> Forgetting all our yesterdays.

October 29 was announced as the crusade's youth day, and the program resembled the earlier event in Cleveland, with Psalty the Singing Songbook delighting thousands of children in the morning and a major youth concert that night. This time dc Talk shared the billing with Take 6, an African American a cappella sextet formed in the early 1980s at Oakwood College, a historically African American Seventh-day Adventist school in Huntsville, Alabama. By 1994, Take 6 boasted multiple Grammys and a diverse crossover following, their sound described by the press as running the gamut from "hard-hitting rhythm and blues to pop balladry and gospel-inflected jazz." Once again Barrows spent a few hours with the musicians before "Jammin' at the Dome" overflowed the stadium's 74,000 seats with an audience mostly under twenty-one. Thousands spilled over onto the playing field, and the crowd of 78,000 broke the Georgia Dome's all-time attendance record (numbering 5,200 more than had attended the 1994 Super Bowl). An intensive high-tech light and laser show apparatus suspended from a sixty-foot-high truss (one of only two in the country) slammed the audience's senses. The show was produced as a labor of love by Scott DeVoss—a convert from Graham's 1987 Denver crusade—whose list of secular music clients included the Rolling Stones, Madonna, Michael Jackson, and Pink Floyd. The crowd swayed and shouted to the ear-splitting rap and jazz blaring into every corner of the stadium. The bands interspersed music with testimony about God's mercy and forgiveness. Singer Toby Mac told the crowd that the only reason dc Talk existed "is that fact that we've asked someone into our lives that has given us such peace that we can't shut up about it." When Graham stepped onstage to deliver his oft-repeated sermon on John 3:16, the musicians embraced him and sat behind him to listen. At the end, 5,422 teenagers crowded around the stage to register a decision for Christ. The next day Johnny and June Carter Cash flew in to provide special music for the final crusade service. When the crusade office tallied the statistics, they learned to their delight that over 19,000 had responded to Graham's invitation, 8,383 of them young people under twenty-five.

In December, the BGEA aired thirty minutes of the Cleveland youth concert nationwide on the Fox Network under the title, "The Works." Combining high-energy music with "biblical straight talk," Graham aspired to test the success of programming whose camera work and editing resembled MTV rather than the usual Graham TV specials. In "The Works," music *was* the message. Graham's five-minute remarks had urgency but seemed to TV critics more like commentary on contemporary Christian living than a robust denunciation of sin.

By the numbers, the crusade youth night format introduced in Cleveland and Atlanta seemed an overwhelming success. It did, however, have its critics inside and outside the BGEA. Those most affected by the change—Barrows and Shea—concurred with the observation in Graham's 1997 autobiography, *Just as I Am*: "Admittedly, it wasn't really my kind of music, nor was it what we have ordinarily featured in our meetings during most of our ministry. But times change. As long as the essential message of the gospel is not obscured or compromised, we must use every legitimate method we can."

Fundamentalists and conservative Christians further from the evangelical center expressed dismay that Graham would feature the lifestyles popular culture embraced. Such people continued to consider the beat, the props, the conduct, and the dress associated with rock music entirely off limits for Christians. Media accelerated musical change and aggravated the seemingly ever-present generation gap, and a segment of conservative Christians proudly chose to be left behind. Many naysayers couched their objections in spiritual terms, finding at stake a battle for nothing less than the souls of youth and the future of the nation. In Schools of Evangelism, Barrows challenged detractors (and himself) to be sure to discern between convictions and pride when it came to music—to ponder whether "giving in" to musical changes really sacrificed convictions or, rather, sacrificed personal pride and preference.

Difficult as it was for them personally to abet such basic changes at the end of their careers, the platform trio of Graham, Barrows, and Shea kept their eyes on the message, stepped back from the limelight, and gained another decade of enthusiastic support from youth. At youth concerts, Graham assumed a grandfatherly role, and in regular crusade meetings, Barrows and Shea seemed to come under his mantle. They had a new form of relevance. Another decade of ministry lay before them, and rather than being old, irrelevant men from another era (as they had seemed to some in the '80s), they gained reputations as legends with wisdom and warm hearts for the next generation. Michael W. Smith commended them, dc Talk made much of their integrity, and the public endorsement and cooperation of such contemporary artists brought young people out in droves to youth concerts and other events.

For the remaining ten years of Billy Graham crusades, the team typically conducted two three-or-four-day crusades each year in a few American cities, and these always included a youth concert. They eventually settled on a brand that brought unity to their youth concerts: each was called a Concert for the NeXt Generation (or, later, Concert for Our Generation). In light of the reshaped nature of the campaigns, Smith, crusade pianist since 1950, relinquished that role to produce crusade events. As Smith assumed his new role, John Innes made a seamless transition from organ to piano.

For a period of ten years, dc Talk and Michael W. Smith headlined most youth nights, but several other popular artists also appeared. In 1999, urban gospel hip-hop artist Kirk Franklin joined dc Talk for a mammoth event in St. Louis. Later in 1999, the rhythm-and-blues sound of Anointed, the alternative pop-rock stylings of Audio Adrenaline, and the anthem-pop sound of Michael W. Smith combined for a concert at the RCA Dome in Indianapolis. Graham called the music and the musicians "his interpreters for today's generation."

Youth concerts routinely set attendance records. At the Metrodome in the Twin Cities in 1996, 82,000 filled every indoor space, while some 12,000 more watched on giant outdoor screens. The next night, Graham broke the Metrodome's attendance record again with 95,000—his largest crusade crowd ever in the United States. Music was surely part of the draw that night, as Barrows allotted multiplatinum Christian pop star Amy Grant (who had only appeared at a crusade in 1979) time for four numbers, including her award-winning rendition of the 1882 hymn "'Tis So Sweet to Trust in Jesus." At the Concert for the NeXt Generation in Tampa in October 1998, young people jammed Raymond James Stadium to hear dc Talk and Jars of Clay, a crossover alternative band that had reached the number twelve slot on *Billboard*'s modern rock chart with their hit single "Flood" in 1995. Altogether, 74,000 were in attendance that evening while another 6,257 participated in a Graham Internet "first" that saw the concert streamed live.

At Graham's June 2000 crusade in "Music City"—Nashville—so many contemporary artists flocked to support the crusade that Barrows turned each evening into a miniconcert by arranging service schedules with generous slots for music—twenty minutes for Michael W. Smith and Band; thirty for the Gaither Vocal Band and Friends (Vestal Goodman, Larnelle Harris, Babbie Mason, the Easters, and more); thirty for country celebrities the Charlie Daniels Band, Connie Smith, Ricky Skaggs, and Marty Stuart; and twenty for CeCe Winans and an accompanying gospel choir. At the Concert for the NeXt Generation, Kirk Franklin, Jars of Clay, and dc Talk rocked the stadium and paid Graham their ultimate compliment by calling him "real." Toby Mac of dc Talk remembered "more than a few raised eyebrows" when his band played its first Graham youth concert six years earlier. Fourteen concerts and scores of thousands of converts later, he praised Graham for ignoring the naysayers who grumbled, "I don't know about this music," and sticking by his resolve to reach youth. "We're finally catching on to what heaven is going to be like," CeCe Winans told a crusade crowd. "There are going to be many different races and many different styles of music."

In November 2000, Graham's calendar included a crusade in Jacksonville, Florida. As opening day neared, though, Graham's health made it unlikely that he could meet his full schedule. He arrived in Jacksonville following a thirteen-week stay at the Mayo Clinic, and organizers announced that he would not appear at the Concert for the NeXt Generation. When the time came, though, Graham showed up at Alltel Stadium, where 70,000 jumping, dancing, clapping, and bopping young people had just enjoyed what the local paper called "a feast of contemporary Christian rock" with Jars of Clay, Kirk Franklin, and dc Talk. Graham's message that night lasted just twenty-four minutes, but it brought 3,650 young people forward for counseling.

The youth concert success continued apace in 2001. The Central Valley Crusade at Fresno's Bulldog Stadium in October shattered local records when Kirk Franklin and dc Talk drew a stadium-record crowd of 47,000 while 15,000 more watched the concert at a nearby baseball complex on giant screens. The 62,000 attendees included the one-millionth person to attend a Concert for the NeXt Generation. "To have an 82-year-old with Parkinson's breaking stadium attendance records with young people—go figure," Graham's publicist A. Larry Ross told the press. In the end—despite illness, accidents, and general frailty—Graham prioritized youth nights and spoke at all twenty-two Concerts for the NeXt Generation. All of these events were free, though a collection was taken at each concert. Most of the artists donated their services, with the crusade meeting their direct expenses. In return, they played the largest live audiences of their careers and benefited from brisk sales of their cassettes and CDs in stadium lobbies.

By the time Concerts for the NeXt Generation began, Graham had cut back on international travel, but his eagerness to preach to all the world and reach out to global youth remained keen. In March 1995, technology stepped up to help by transforming Hiram Bithorn Stadium, an eighteen-thousand-seat baseball venue in San Juan, Puerto Rico, into a global pulpit. Graham's team reimagined the three-day crusade as a massive media event—the largest evangelistic endeavor in history. Workers brought in miles of cable and transformed San Juan's Roberto Clemente Coliseum into a media production center. Video carried services from Hiram Bithorn Stadium to the Coliseum, where forty-eight interpreters translated Graham's preaching into the world's major languages. Professionals then packaged video, audio, and prepared music and testimonies with the service and transmitted via a network of thirty satellites to 185 countries across twenty-nine time zones. At some locations, people stood by to translate the sermon into sixty-eight additional local languages and dialects. The remote revival centers ranged from hillsides in refugee camps to city squares and sports arenas, and in each place, counselors trained by the BGEA waited to reap the harvest. The potential audience numbered one billion, or more than one-fifth of the world's population. The *New York Times* cited statistics indicating that Graham's prior satellite preaching brought 14 percent of the audience to a decision, a number that exceeded average audience responses to his in-person delivery.

The team targeted under-thirties as the audience for global mission, and as a result, decisions about music proved controversial from the outset. The BGEA customized a twenty-five-minute film package for eight global regions, selecting culturally appropriate testimonies and music they believed would reach a young audience. The choices for English speakers were clearly influenced by the recent changes in youth concert music; some took offense or simply opted out of the presermon part of the event, while others welcomed the music from longtime British rocker Sir Cliff Richard and the American bands Take 6 and dc Talk that interspersed testimonies from Jimmy Carter, Elizabeth Dole, and British track star Kriss Akabusi. On each of the three evenings, Barrows delivered his opening remarks flanked by a different contemporary singer (Steve Green, Michael W. Smith, and Filipino singing star Gary Valenciano), and each followed the remarks with a song. Barrows's welcome and the presermon solo by Shea were all that remained of the traditional presermon crusade sound and ritual.

The changes in crusade music from the late 1980s forward undeniably gave greater visibility to CCM, but they were also consistent with the principles that had guided crusade music all along. From 1949, crusades had featured popular Christian artists. Generational change brought along both new artists and newer sounds. The basic challenge to every artist remained exactly the same: deliver a clear gospel message. Just as Ethel Waters, Wilmos Csehy, or Jerome Hines had had the cultural presence to attract crowds at the outset, so Michael W. Smith, dc Talk, and Kirk Franklin did so toward the end.

Barrows and Shea remained fixtures and legends, as each dealt with increasing frailty. A Lubbock, Texas, reporter noted that Graham, Barrows, and Shea went together "like love and marriage or H. and R. Block"—one did not come without the other, and as the three aged, some admitted attending crusades as much to pay personal tribute to them as to participate in an evangelistic opportunity. In 1989, Barrows underwent surgery to remove a nerve in his right ear, losing his hearing in that ear, and he missed two crusades. In the '90s, his eyesight began to fail. Shea no longer had the stamina to sing more than once in a service or the breath to hold out his notes. A mild heart attack in the late '90s broke his fifty-year perfect attendance record at domestic crusades. Yet people expected their physical presence and participation: they had become as much part of the crusade experience as the evangelist himself, but they could no longer carry the full load. Others came alongside to rehearse the mass choirs and to provide a larger share of the special music. Shea's repertoire did not change, nor did Barrows's selection preferences for choir and congregational songs. The new sounds came through a new generation of guest artists.

Onetime pianist Tedd Smith, now crusade production manager, made possible the contemporary music parts of crusades, from youth nights to regular services, by working closely with the artists and their backup people to understand their setup requirements and rehearsal needs. He had guided selections and rehearsed with artists before, but his new role relieved Barrows from attending to the myriad of expanded details the new media-driven approach required. Smith had a free hand in planning youth nights, a task he fulfilled until 2004 when, after fifty-four years of service, an attempt to restrict his freedom led to his resignation barely a year before the final crusade.

In general, then, contemporary music at crusades mirrored changing times and technology. In the 1950s there was, perhaps, less difference between the repertoires of guest artists and those Shea and Barrows favored. But by the 1990s, a marked difference in musical styles made crusades seem rather like the blended services that increasingly reflected the reality in many of the nation's congregations. Encouragement from some in the BGEA to completely alter the signature sound failed. Graham preferred to avoid conflict, but through it all he recognized—as he had since the beginning—that Barrows's song leading, mass choirs, certain congregational songs, and Shea solos were iconic and indispensable elements of the crusade sound.

CODA

I n late June 2005 the final Billy Graham crusade was held in New York City. The venue was Flushing Meadows–Corona Park in Queens, the site of the 1964 World's Fair: the location was fitting. The BGEA had a visible presence at that World's Fair in the form of a pavilion that highlighted Graham's growing international ministry. The pavilion also provided continuous showings of *Man in the Fifth Dimension*, a half-hour film featuring an evangelistic pitch from Graham undergirded by a score by renowned Hollywood pop composer, arranger, and producer Ralph Carmichael. Flushing Meadows was likewise but a few miles away from Madison Square Garden, site of his groundbreaking 1957 New York crusade. That crusade had cemented Graham's position as the nation's preeminent evangelical voice and introduced the nation—and the world—to Bev Shea's iconic rendition of "How Great Thou Art." It was also at that crusade that Cliff Barrows had persuaded Ethel Waters to step forward and share her testimony in singing "His Eye Is on the Sparrow." Although Graham in many ways embodied the evangelical Christian voice of America's heartland, the symbolic importance of New York City in the history of the Graham team's story made it an ideal choice for its final chapter.

Over the course of the three-day event, more than 240,000 people were in attendance while hundreds of reporters and media outlets from around the world covered the crusade. The crusade location was one of the most ethnically diverse sections of New York, and Graham's sermons were translated into thirteen different languages. The eighty-six-year-old Graham steered away, as he had for many years, from politics and controversy and centered on the basics of the gospel message in his sermons. His main theme was the abiding love of Christ, but on the final night, in a sermon on Noah, he reminded the audience that the world system's time was short, and that Jesus's return was close at hand. All in all, an estimated 9,400 responded to Graham's appeals and "gave their hearts to Jesus."

As it had always done through the years, music played an important part in the 2005 New York City crusade. The decades-long changes in the crusades' musical sound and the diversity of its many supportive publics were on prominent display. A slew of prominent featured artists spoke to this evolution, including Michael W. Smith, Steven Curtis Chapman, Jars of Clay, Salvador, Nicole C. Mullen, MercyMe, the Brooklyn Tabernacle Choir, and the Gaither Vocal Band.

Nonetheless, the old hymns and gospel songs and the 1,200-voice crusade choir still anchored the musical center and struck a responsive chord. Barrows, comparatively spry at eighty-two, lent energy and joy to leading the audience and choir in song. Shea, now ninety-six years old and challenged by diminished lung capacity, soldiered on and gave credible renditions of "How Great Thou Art" at each service. Hearkening back to the early days of the crusade ministry, after each meeting there were reports of the audience leaving the meetings filling subway cars with song.

One of the highlights of this final crusade was a poignant moment when Graham asked Shea and Barrows to join him at the podium. The "cord of three," linked in purpose, calling, and ministry since the late 1940s, stood together once again. Graham publicly thanked them for being his partners in supporting his ministry, grateful that "they put up with me for the sixty years we've been together." The audience gave them a rousing, and heartfelt, ovation.

On the final day of the New York crusade, Graham concluded his message with a simple call to action to the sixty thousand–plus in attendance: "The Bible says today is the accepted time. Today is the day of salvation." At that moment, Barrows turned toward the crusade choir, raised his arms, and launched the singers—as he had done for nearly sixty years—into the familiar strains of song inviting the troubled of heart and sin-weary hearers to come:

> Just as I am, without one plea,
> But that Thy blood was shed for me.
> And that Thou bid'st me come to Thee,
> O Lamb of God, I come, I come.

SELECT BIBLIOGRAPHY

Blumhofer, Edith L. *Her Heart Can See: The Life and Hymns of Fanny Crosby*. Library of Religious Biography. Grand Rapids: Eerdmans, 2005.

———. "Singing to Save: Music in the Billy Graham Crusades." In *Billy Graham: American Pilgrim*, edited by Andrew Finstuen, Grant Wacker, and Anne Blue Wills. New York: Oxford University Press, 2017.

Bohlman, Philip V., Edith L. Blumhofer, and Maria M. Chow, eds. *Music in American Religious Experience*. New York: Oxford University Press, 2005.

Carpenter, Joel A. *Revive Us Again: The Reawakening of American Fundamentalism*. New York: Oxford University Press, 1997.

Cusic, Don. *The Sound of Light: A History of Gospel and Christian Music*. Milwaukee: Hal Leonard Corp., 2002.

Davis, Paul. *George Beverly Shea: Tell Me the Story*. Greenville, SC: Ambassador International, 2009.

Enss, Chris, and Howard Kazanjian. *The Cowboy and the Senorita: A Biography of Roy Rogers and Dale Evans*. Guilford, CT: TwoDot Books, 2004.

Gaither, Bill, with Ken Abraham. *It's More Than the Music: Life Lessons on Friends, Faith, and What Matters Most*. New York: Time Warner Books, 2003.

Graham, Billy. *Just as I Am: The Autobiography of Billy Graham*. New York: HarperOne, 1997.

Harper, Redd. *I Walk the Glory Road: An Autobiography by Redd Harper*. Woodlawn, NJ: Revell, 1957.

Larson, Mel. *Young Man on Fire: The Story of Torrey Johnson and Youth for Christ*. Chicago: Youth Publications, 1945; reprint, Kessinger Publishing, 2008.

Martin, William. *A Prophet with Honor: The Billy Graham Story*. Updated ed. Grand Rapids: Zondervan, 2018.

Mitchell, Curtis. *God in the Garden: The Story of Billy Graham's First New York Crusade.* New York: Doubleday, 1957; commemorative ed., Billy Graham Evangelistic Association, 2005.

Mungons, Kevin. *Homer Rodeheaver and the Rise of the Gospel Music Industry.* Music in American Life. Urbana: University of Illinois Press, 2021.

Pollock, John. *Billy Graham, Evangelist to the World: An Authorized Biography of the Decisive Years.* New York: Harper & Row, 1979.

Posner, Steven, and Amy Newmark. *Chicken Soup for the Soul: Billy Graham and Me; 101 Inspiring Stories from Presidents, Pastors, Performers, and Other People Who Know Him Well.* Cos Cob, CT: Chicken Soup for the Soul Publishing, 2013.

Ruth, Lester, and Lim Swee Hong. *A History of Contemporary Praise & Worship: Understanding the Ideas That Reshaped the Protestant Church.* Grand Rapids: Baker Academic, 2021.

Shea, George Beverly. *How Sweet the Sound; Amazing Stories and Grace-Filled Reflections on Beloved Hymns and Gospel Songs.* Wheaton, IL: Tyndale House, 2004.

Stanley, Brian. *The Global Diffusion of Evangelicalism: The Age of Billy Graham and John Stott.* History of Evangelicalism, vol. 5. Downers Grove, IL: IVP Academic, 2013.

Turner, Steve. *The Man Called Cash: The Life, Love, and Faith of an American Legend.* London: Bloomsbury, 2005.

Wacker, Grant. *America's Pastor: Billy Graham and the Shaping of a Nation.* Cambridge, MA: Belknap Press of Harvard University Press, 2014.

Waters, Ethel. *To Me It's Wonderful.* New York: Harper Books, 1972.

INDEX OF NAMES AND SUBJECTS

INDEX OF SONGS